THE EAGLE AND THE RISING SUN

America
and Japan
in the
Twentieth
Century

John K. Emmerson
Harrison M. Holland

FORT MY

A Portable Stanford Book

Addison-Wesley Publishing Company, Inc.
Massachusetts   Menlo Park, California   New York
Don Mills, Ontario   Wokingham, England   Amsterdam   Bonn
Sydney   Singapore   Tokyo   Madrid   San Juan

This edition is published by arrangement
with the Stanford Alumni Association.

*Library of Congress Cataloging-in-
Publication Data*

Emmerson, John K.
  The eagle and the rising sun.

  "A Portable Stanford book."
  Bibliography: p.
  Includes index.
    1. United States—Relations—Japan.
  2. Japan—Relations—United States.
  3. United States—Foreign relations—
  20th century. 4. Japan—Foreign
  relations—20th century. I. Holland,
  Harrison M., 1921–   . II. Title.
  E183.8.J3E48   1988
  303.4'8252'073   87-38505
  ISBN 0-201-08891-6

Cover design by Jeffrey Whitten
Text design and calligraphy by Yumiko Ready

ABCDEFGHIJ-DO-898
First printing, February 1988

THE
EAGLE
AND
THE
RISING
SUN

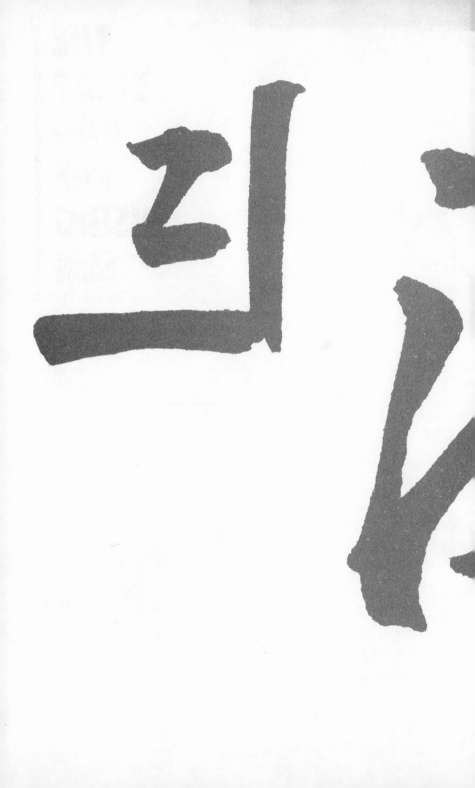

CONTENTS ∎

J ohn Emmerson and I spent many years in Japan as Foreign Service officers and witnessed many of the phenomenal changes that took place as the country rebuilt its cities, towns, and factories destroyed by war. We wish to share with the reader some of our observations about Japanese institutions and history: how these two Pacific nations, the United States and Japan, began their relationship, how that relationship was ravaged by war and rebuilt during the occupation and its aftermath, and how Japan emerged in the 1960s and beyond as the chief challenger to American worldwide economic dominance. In spite of their marked contrasts—value systems that derive from diverse historical backgrounds, deep cultural differences, and differing attitudes about the role each should assume in this dangerous world— these two great nations have been able to forge an alliance that has netted a degree of both peace and prosperity that is the envy of friend and foe. At this point, however, the U.S.-Japan alliance, born in adversity and bonded through the recognition of shared interests, is facing one of its most serious postwar tests.

The Eagle and the Rising Sun is for the general reader. It is not intended as an archival presen-

A WORD FROM THE AUTHORS 1

tation. Its purpose is to clear up some of the misunderstandings that have arisen in the alliance, principally over trade and defense. The book recalls some of the highlights of Japan's early history, the geographic and cultural influences that conditioned Japan's modern development, and how U.S.-Japan relations have evolved in the post-World War II period. It focuses on the critical trade and security issues, the rivalry that has become almost endemic between the United States and Japan; comments on Japan's contemporary relations with the Soviet Union, the People's Republic of China, and the Republic of Korea, and their effect on her relations with the United States; and prognosticates on Japan's intentions to play a more influential role in international affairs.

Much has been written about postwar U.S.-Japan relations, yet there continues to be considerable misunderstanding about the role and responsibilities of each country in the relationship. While paying considerable attention to the controversial trade issue, we also argue that, despite the differences that divide the United States and Japan, the relationship is not only important to both countries but plays a key role in maintaining economic viability and peace in the Pacific Basin.

The authors have taken the position that changes in economic, financial, and trade policies of both nations are necessary to alleviate friction caused by Japan's growing trade surpluses with the United States. Hand-in-hand with policy changes must go greater efforts by each country to better understand the other. The United States could begin by gaining greater appreciation for the constraints on Japanese security; for the economic and financial imperatives in Japanese policy; for the social and cultural forces that are slowing Japan's efforts to assume a greater international role; and for the impulses moving Japan in her relations with the Soviet Union, the People's Republic of China, and the Republic of Korea.

Japan must try harder to grasp some of the imperatives in U.S. policy opposing Japanese trade and security practices. Patience, tolerance, and common sense—virtues not always present in a dynamic relationship between countries with such different cultures and political and economic systems—are more necessary today than ever before, as strains in U.S.-Japan relations continue to grow.

The book presses for a heightened awareness of the values that motivate the two cultures, for a realistic approach to solutions of security and economic problems, for avoidance of emotional and subjective judgment in reacting to policy differences, and for an appreciation of the importance of the alliance to basic U.S. security interests in the Western Pacific.

The authors have striven to give the reader a feeling for the immense changes wrought by the Japanese people themselves in building a modern nation out of the dust of total defeat. Their cities display buildings of exciting architectural design and a transportation system that is second to none in the world; huge factory complexes pour out goods that are exported to all corners of the world and have made Japan the leading creditor nation; and great universities continue to enrich Japanese society. A highly disciplined, educated, and homogeneous society has made all this possible, yet the country is introspective and continues to be unsure of what the future holds. Having observed many of these changes, it is our hope that by bringing them alive for the reader, we will create a better understanding of the importance of this troubled alliance to the welfare and security of both nations.

Half completed at the time of his death on March 24, 1984, this book was begun by John K. Emmerson, a distinguished diplomat and scholar. Asked by the Emmerson family to complete the manuscript, I welcomed the opportunity. John was my friend, a colleague in the U.S. Foreign Service, and a contemporary at the Northeast Asia–United States Forum on International Policy at Stanford University and at the Hoover Institution.

I wish to acknowledge with deep appreciation the support I have received from the Emmerson family; from Claude Buss, Emeritus Professor of History, Stanford University; from Miriam Miller, editor, and from Gayle Hemenway, production coordinator, of Portable Stanford; and from my colleagues at the Northeast Asia–United States Forum on International Policy.

John Emmerson was a firm believer in the importance of creating better understanding between Japan and the United States. But he was no visionary. He was realistic and objective in assessing the strengths and weaknesses in the U.S.-Japan alliance and was a strong voice for reason and tolerance. This book reflects such a philosophy. It is a final literary tribute to John K. Emmerson, a quiet, scholarly, good man who devoted most of his life to the promotion of better understanding between Japan and the United States.

Harrison M. Holland

Stanford, California

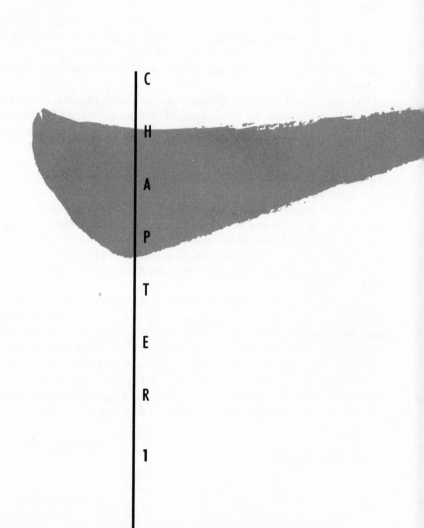

CHAPTER 1

The United States and Japan, one nation born a mere two centuries ago and the other emerging out of a cloudy antiquity, have come to a relationship as important as that between any two countries in the world.

Contrasts between Japan and the United States are startling and the association of these two Pacific neighbors, short from the prospect of recorded time, has been turbulent. The history and differences go far to explain the problems and prospects of what has come to be termed a Japanese-American "partnership," only recently winning acceptance by both Japanese and Americans as a full-fledged alliance.

Several factors are basic to any discussion of Japanese-American relations: Japan is an island nation, the United Sates is continental. The area of the United States is nearly twenty-five times that of Japan, which is roughly the size of the state of Montana. From the beginning of man's memory, Japan has been visited by disasters: volcanoes, earthquakes, fires, floods, and typhoons, to which in certain centuries were added clashes of arms in bloody internecine warfare.

The climax to all these natural and man-made tragedies came in World War II when Japan suffered atomic attack. Out of this suffer-

THE
TROUBLED
ALLIANCE

ing from the prevalence and frequency of disaster, explained by Buddhist teachings as manifestations of the inevitability of all things, has come a strain of stoicism in the Japanese character, a certain acceptance of life as it comes. The effects of war with the United States, prefaced by ten years of fighting on the China mainland and Southeast Asian territories, made postwar generations profoundly pacifist and determined that war would never again come to their country.

The United States has escaped the traumas that have afflicted Japan. While geography and history have forced Japan to look inward (although its trade has penetrated to the farthest nations), the United States borders two oceans and its interests gird the globe. The differences in these horizons form a major theme in understanding both the interdependence and the difficulties that characterize the relationship between the United States and Japan.

If not managed with skill and understanding, the troubled alliance between Japan and the United States carries perils for both nations. In the decades since World War II, the Japanese challenge to American economic dominance has grown almost geometrically and has now created economic, political, and philosophical conditions that are taxing the viability and strength of the alliance. Competition between these two great Pacific nations is turning adversarial, so that rivalry rather than accommodation sets the tone. The drift toward confrontation holds dangers for the economies of both countries, imperils their relationship, and has uncertain consequences for peace and security in the Western Pacific.

Today the Japan-United States relationship is beset by two critical problems, trade and defense. The ability of Japan and the United States to deal successfully with the underlying causes of these issues will determine the basic nature of the partnership for years to come. Of the two, trade is less important to the ultimate health and viability of the relationship than defense. For the present, however, the trade issue overshadows security and is the cause of growing tension between the two countries.

The extent of Japan's anxiety and resentment was recently brought home to me rather forcefully as I talked to an old Japanese friend in Tokyo. He expressed deep concern that continued criticism of Japanese trade and security policies by the United States might eventually lead to a serious impasse in relations. He was especially worried that if "Japan-bashing," whether a current fad or prompted by sincere conviction, were not checked, serious harm could come to U.S.-Japan economic and security interests. Rising tensions in his own country over Washington's accusations that Japan engages in unfair trade practices and was getting a "free ride" on defense, he asserted, were taking a heavy toll on the nerves of the Japanese people and could cause growing resentment against the United States.

My friend's concern is shared by many sensitive and knowledgeable Japanese, who are torn between a strong sense of national pride that takes umbrage at what is considered undeserved criticism, and the reality of Japan's geopolitical position in Asia, her dependence on imports of food, raw materials, and energy for survival. The legacy of dependence on the United States for security adds a further complication.

The United States, too, has much to worry about if the alliance is weakened by mistrust and intolerance. Japan provides thousands of jobs for Americans, helps to finance the growing U.S. public debt, and gives American consumers high quality and fairly priced products. Moreover, it provides strategic bases for American military forces.

The alliance, characterized by our ambassador to Japan, Mike Mansfield, as the most important bilateral relationship in the world, is fundamentally sound, having grown and prospered out of recognition that it reflected the common interests of both countries. With the current rash of criticism from both sides, however, one is often tempted to overlook the strengths in the relationship: Corporate alliances; cultural and educational links; technology transfers; cooperation in preserving the environment, improving communication, and combining efforts in health research are a few examples of the vitality of the alliance.

In spite of these pluses, however, U.S.-Japan relations are being tested today as never before. Some in the United States see Japan as a threat to their own special interests. One has only to listen to the intemperate language of some congressmen, senators, business executives, and labor leaders to realize how determined they are to pursue their private aims at the expense of the national interest. One wonders how Americans would react to similar remarks from Japanese Diet members. One is also left to speculate whether these American politicians are bent upon undermining an economic relationship that has brought jobs and prosperity to many Americans and weakening a security arrangement that has proven vital to the preservation of peace and stability in the Western Pacific.

The Japanese, a proud and highly nationalistic people, are, as one might expect, growing increasingly resentful of the picture drawn of them as economic animals determined to win by mercantilist means what they were unable to achieve by military means. Yet they too have indulged in strong words, characterizing the United States as a bully, not averse to throwing illegal punches, and determined to make Japan the scapegoat for failures of Reagan economic policies and for the declining competitiveness of American industry.

One could hardly have foreseen such a turn in the relationship when the occupation ended and the Japanese embarked on the difficult task of rebuilding their shattered nation. When I first arrived in Japan in January 1954, attention was focused mainly on the security question. The Japanese constitution, which had been written in General Douglas MacArthur's headquarters, called for a totally disarmed Japan, with strict prohibition on the development of all offensive weapons, and declared in Article 9 that Japan renounced war as an instrument of national policy. Most Japanese greeted the new constitution with enthusiasm and to date not one word of the American-drafted document has been changed. It was therefore bewildering to most Japanese when Vice President Richard Nixon visited Japan in 1953 and urged the Japanese to begin to rearm. The United States has followed this general policy line ever since.

From 1954 until 1960, the main issue in U.S.-Japan relations was security. Many in Japan had grown resentful of the privileges afforded U.S. military forces in Japan as a result of the first mutual security treaty signed on September 8, 1951, and pressures mounted for modification. One of my first assignments as a young political officer was to prepare reports on public attitudes in the Kobe/Osaka area toward rearmament and revision of the existing security treaty; I found the public temper overwhelmingly for change.

Pressures continued to grow, and in June 1957 Prime Minister Kishi and President Eisenhower agreed that all American combat forces would be withdrawn from Japan. As negotiations continued over treaty revision, it was clear that a major adjustment in U.S.-Japan security relations was near. After careful and often wearying negotiations, a new mutual security treaty was signed in January 1960 and the great treaty crisis began. It was to be a watershed in postwar Japanese history. Socialists, Communists, labor unions, leftist intellectuals, and radical student groups combined to rampage through Tokyo and other major cities demanding the resignation of Prime Minister Kishi, the scrapping of the Mutual Security Treaty, and the withdrawal of the invitation to President Eisenhower to visit Japan. Motivations for demonstrations were mixed. The progressives were after Kishi's political scalp, complaining that he had "rammed" the treaty through the Diet without giving the opposition an opportunity to be heard. The Communists and left-wing Socialists also wanted to embarrass the government by forcing Kishi to withdraw the invitation to Eisenhower to visit Japan.

Despite the turmoil, the treaty was finally ratified by the Japanese Diet on June 19, 1960. Four days later Prime Minister Kishi was compelled to resign. He was succeeded by Ikeda Hayato, who immediately decided that Japan would adopt a policy of "low posture" on defense, concentrating instead on economic development. This was the beginning of the famous Ikeda "income-doubling" program that led ultimately to the great Japanese "economic miracle"—a policy, driven by a mercantilist philosophy, that sowed the seeds of the present controversy over trade between Japan and the United States.

This was the period when John Emmerson and I were in the embassy in Tokyo and were, in a sense, in on the beginning of this great Japanese economic experiment. An early harbinger of Japanese determination to build an economic colossus was their success in preparing for the Olympic Games held in Tokyo in 1964. The Japanese literally rebuilt their city to accommodate the tens of thousands of visitors from abroad, a remarkable feat made all the more astonishing by the rapidity with which the Japanese changed the face of their capital city: One day a famous landmark was there; the next day it was gone, replaced by a new building or a broadened road. It was indeed a portend of things to come, of a Japan transforming itself into a showplace for the overseas visitor to admire, gaining respect for achievement, and nurturing inherent Japanese pride.

Although the challenge to U.S. trade dominance was in its infancy at that time, the signs were unmistakable—Japan was beginning to move on the trade front. Few then could have foreseen the immensity of the challenge. It was not until the 1970s that Japanese automobiles, TV sets, and other electronic products began to make serious inroads into the American market, creating problems for American companies, arousing strong congressional sentiment, and heralding the era of "Japan-bashing." Today, the call for protectionism has reached the point where the U.S. Congress is considering highly restrictive trade legislation pointed primarily at Japan.

It is sobering to consider where all this might lead if misunderstandings grow and tolerance becomes an object of derision. The consequences for both countries could be appalling. Consider the reaction of the hundreds of thousands of American workers and companies who have forged successful links with Japanese enterprises—and depend on these enterprises for their livelihood—if links were weakened or severed. California alone supplies most of Japan's food imports. Two-way trade has already surpassed $100 billion annually and continues to grow.

Think of the repercussions for America's friends in Asia were Japan to deny us the use of its military bases; of the tremendous opportunity this would afford the Soviet Union to extend its influence at the expense of the United States. A security relationship that has meant stability and peace in Northeast Asia for over three decades cannot be easily dismissed in the heat of controversy as merely providing Japan a "free ride." Japanese bases used by U.S. military forces and supported by an annual $1 billion contribution from the Japanese government have checked Soviet adventurism, provided the Chinese with a psychological backstop for their continuing problems with the Russians, and brought a sort of modus vivendi to relations between North and South Korea.

Consider what would happen to the Treasury Department's ability to pay off government obligations if it had no Japanese customers for Treasury bonds. On the Japanese side, think of the upheaval that would occur if America's markets were closed to Japanese products— rising unemployment, social tension, political instability, and a sense of isolation that could lead, as in the past, to unpredictable lurches in Japanese foreign policy.

To defuse growing tensions and reduce the level of acrimony will be difficult. Both countries are, in a sense, locked in the prison of the past. Japan's huge trade surplus is generally believed caused by an archaic financial system that was created during the period of underdevelopment but in the 1980s is promoting surging Japanese exports and restraining domestic expansion.

For the United States, conditioned to being dominant in international trade and commerce, resentment of Japan's success has literally become an obsession that is blinding us to the realities of our mutual interests. The solution to our problems with Japan, say the "experts," is for Japan to restructure its economy, overhaul its financial system, allow unrestricted importation of American cigarettes, and buy American cars even though the steering wheel is on the wrong side. To many Japanese these demands read like a series of directives from General MacArthur's headquarters. But the occupation of Japan is over and we should be thinking about how to solve our problems as equal partners and not in an *oyabun-kobun* (leader-follower) relationship of years gone by.

We might start by paying some attention to what the United States needs to do to get its own economic house in order: attack the budget deficit, change the tax laws to encourage rather than penalize savers, increase productivity, improve marketing techniques, invest more in technological innovation, and strengthen labor-management relations.

The Japanese could help their own cause by not selling sensitive technology to the Soviet Union, by giving American companies equal bidding rights with Japanese corporations for work on the new Osaka International Airport, by ceasing to dump some of their products on the U.S. market, and by making their domestic markets more open and flexible.

These measures are imperative for both sides if we are to arrest the deterioration in U.S.-Japan relations. Yet, for the U.S. Congress, the answer to the U.S.-Japan trade problem seems to be to enact an omnibus, protectionist trade bill, clearly directed at Japan, that would damage the U.S. economy and hurt the consumer. From Japan, there are many promises but few measurable results.

Pending the reformation of human nature, Japan and the United States will continue to have troubles in their alliance. As we have noted, too many cultural differences, value systems that derive from diverse historical backgrounds, and differing attitudes about the roles each should assume in international society make it unrealistic to predict smooth sailing. But the relationship has survived disquieting times before (the 1960 rioting over the renewal of the U.S.-Japan Mutual Security Treaty is one example), because both countries recognized their common interest in maintaining workable trade and security relations.

While the trade issue is currently in the spotlight, defense is more fundamental to the ultimate health of the alliance. Although manageable at present, defense could develop into a knotty problem, especially if it were too closely linked to trade or to any shift in American defense policy in Northeast Asia. Trade and defense are, unfortunately, often linked, particularly by critics who advance the argument that Japan has been getting a "free ride" at the expense of the United States, inasmuch as we guarantee its security. Such linkage introduces a political element that tends to exacerbate the relationship instead of placing emphasis on the solution of specific problems on their merits. Americans must remember that the United States wrote the constitution that prohibits the creation of Japanese military forces, and that present—and contradictory—U.S. insistence on Japanese rearmament has added to confusion in the Japanese mind. When called upon, early on, to defend the creation of the Self Defense Forces in the face of criticism from Japan's neighbors and "progressive" political elements inside Japan, the Japanese government made the case that the United Nations Charter gives each sovereign state the right of self-defense.

It is important, too, for Americans to understand that Japan's defense policy is constrained within certain legal and political boundaries, the force and nature of which many foreigners do not understand. Japan has been able to conduct its defense establishment through interpretation rather than through strict observance of these constraints. Japan's defense policy is based on the premise that Japan is not threatened by anyone and therefore need not increase her military strength at a pace that would impinge on economic development or the "comfortable life" increasingly enjoyed by the Japanese people. A complicating factor is that Japan views its defense strategy in regional terms, whereas the United States looks upon its security interests in global dimensions.

In addition to these broad policy differences, other considerations have influenced Japanese defense policy: Japan's strict adherence to the constitution, a document generally acknowledged to have been written by U.S. occupation authorities, and to its Article 9, which renounces war as an instrument of national policy. Laws prohibit the possession, manufacture, or introduction of nuclear weapons in Japan; provide for the adoption of a strictly defensive military posture; ban the export of military equipment; and limit defense expenditures to 1 percent of the Gross National Product. A small breach has been made in the 1 percent limit in the FY (fiscal year) 1987 national budget, with military expenditures slightly exceeding 1 percent of GNP to an estimated figure of 1.004 percent. Even this small increase has brought cries of militarism and accusations of a disregard of the constitution by opposition parties. It has also brought charges from the United States that 1 percent of GNP is insufficient for Japan to carry her part of the responsibility for defense.

Still other limitations on Japan's defense efforts are her delicate financial situation (her cumulative budget deficit is approaching $600 billion or over 40 percent of her GNP); the lack of a realistic blueprint for a defense buildup; the bureaucratic weakness of the Japan Defense Agency (JDA); her ostensible concern about the reaction of her neighbors to an ambitious defense program; the public's perception of the "threat" which tends to put JDA officials on the defensive; and—the most formidable obstacle of all—public opinion, which will support only a modest defense effort.

These constraints, together with restrictions imposed by constitutional and legal considerations, are slowing the pace of Japan's defense buildup program and complicating U.S.-Japan security relations. Given the public's deep antipathy to militarism, which is daily fed by the major newspapers, and the reluctance of leaders of the ruling Liberal Democratic party to guide the defense debate into more productive channels, progress in the defense program will be slow and measured. The United States can do little to force the pace until a consensus forms in Japan to allow for greater accceleration of the defense buildup effort.

Added to this anti-militarist feeling is an insular mentality that makes Japanese reluctant to become too involved in international affairs. Yet pressures on Japan to assume greater global responsibility are growing and are causing Japan to examine the costs and benefits of internationalization for them and their country by engaging in a sort of self-analysis.

The term "internationalization of Japan" is an oft-used code phrase that means different things to different people. It is now popular terminology in Japan and connotes a new frontier toward which the Japanese believe they must travel to satisfy their longing for recognition as a major world power. But for most Japanese the drive for international recognition is painful. Japan has lived with a legacy of geographic and political isolation and this has bred an insularity in the Japanese psyche that makes them suspicious of outsiders. The word *gaijin*, or foreign person, is used liberally by Japanese and carries a certain innuendo that foreigners who live and work in Japan feel. Japan's spectacular success in international trade and commerce has done little to diminish her belief in her own uniqueness, or the conviction of outsiders that Japan is inbred and culturally alienated from the rest of the world.

Low posture and reactive diplomacy have been the norm for Japan's postwar foreign relations. Her sensitivity to any actions that might disrupt her international trade patterns has been the essential guide for her participation in world affairs. Despite her awesome economic power and her position today as the major creditor nation, Japan has been hesitant to assert a positive role in international affairs. She has been content, instead, to follow the lead of the United States in major decisions affecting East-West relations.

The United States has urged Japan to be more assertive, to assume more responsibility, as befits a major economic power. Thus far, however, the Japanese have not figured out how to become a global force without scaring themselves and everyone else. Japanese leaders talk a good deal about traditional values and a renewal of the Japanese spirit. Some foreigners, hearing these things, wonder whether Japan is moving back toward prewar days when the emperor was venerated and *bushido*, the spirit of the warrior, was in vogue. ASEAN (Association of Southeast Asian Nations) countries worry about this and so do many Japanese.

Despite the national angst over a high international profile, there is a slow, steady trend toward accepting the reality of a larger role for Japan in international affairs. The course Japan has chosen to follow for her advance onto the international stage has not been determined without substantial prodding from the outside world. As Japan continues to extend her economic reach, she seems to be making greater efforts to understand her neighbors, to give aid to less developed countries, to take initiatives in the political sphere—most notably her support for the Western response to the Rangoon bombings by North Korean extremists, the shootdown of a Korean Air Line (KAL) passenger aircraft by Soviet fighter planes, the invasion of Afghanistan by the Soviet Union and of Cambodia by Vietnamese Communist military forces, and the sanctions against Poland. She is attempting to overcome personal feelings of insecurity; to understand that her success creates jealousy and animosity; and to cope with the realities of her prominent economic position in the family of nations. Having been an international shut-in for many years, Japan has a long way to go to understand the world outside. But available evidence suggests that a consensus is growing in Japanese society that it is a burden that must be borne, however challenging it may be to built-in beliefs and painful to age-old values and cultural traditions.

Japan recognizes that a more active international role will require a keener insight into the policies that motivate her neighbors—the Soviet Union, the People's Republic of China (PRC), and the Republic of Korea (ROK)—and how such policies will affect the U.S.-Japan alliance. Up to now no serious difficulties for the alliance have occurred, but both countries are aware of the potential problems that would lie in wait should there be a shift in Russian, Chinese, or Korean policies toward Japan or the U.S. Japan's relations with her neighbors, her response to the foreign policy initiatives of the PRC, the USSR, and the ROK, and how she rationalizes her trade and security policies with the U.S. in light of these initiatives, are all of special significance in understanding the permutations in the U.S.-Japan partnership.

Since the end of World War II, Japan has been especially sensitive and responsive to changes in her relations with these countries. Her leaders have been particularly concerned about international and regional developments that affect Japan's security and trade with her principal neighbors and her political stability in Northeast Asia, and how these considerations impact on her primary relationship with the United States.

Historically, the Japanese have not gotten on well with the Russians. In the post-World War II era, pragmatism, not ideology, has been the main feature of Russian policy toward Japan, while the Japanese have responded with wariness and concern over the foreign policy demands of their Eurasian neighbor. No peace treaty has been signed, and the Soviets continue to occupy four islands in the Southern Kurile chain: the Habomai group, Shikotan, Kunashiri, and Etorofu, ceded to them at Yalta but claimed by Japan as historically Japanese territory. Despite the strong desire of Japan to have the Northern Islands returned, the Russians refuse to discuss the issue. The Japanese, for their part, mindful of growing Russian military power in the area, are careful not to antagonize the Soviets. Recent moves by the USSR to improve relations with Japan have been largely cosmetic and have had little impact in Japan or on the U.S.-Japan alliance. If the Soviet Union should agree to return the disputed islands to Japan and a peace treaty between the two nations ensue—possibilities presently considered unlikely—such a policy development would be viewed with concern by China and Korea and cause some trepidation in Washington.

A concerted effort by the Russians to improve relations with Japan by conceding the Northern Islands would be taken only if the USSR believed that by doing so it could isolate Japan from the United States, worry the Chinese into engaging in dialogues to restore amicable relations, and force the Republic of Korea into a more accommodating posture toward North Korea.

The United States, for its part, realizes that opportunities for Soviet mischief in the area would be considerably enhanced should the USSR decide to adopt a more amicable and flexible policy toward Japan. Soviet leader Mikhail Gorbachev, in his Vladivostok speech in the summer of 1986, outlining the Soviet Union's campaign for increasing its influence throughout Asia, hinted of things to come, and his words should be taken as a warning to the United States and Japan to bury the trade hatchet and recognize that the Soviet Union intends to become a major player in Asian politics.

Japan's relations with the People's Republic of China also have significance for her relations with the United States, but unlike her relations with the Soviet Union, are weighted more heavily in the economic than in the security area. The likelihood of Japan moving independently of the United States in her China policy is remote. Yet strong economic drives by Japan to corner the China market could heighten competition with the United States, allowing the Chinese to play one off against the other. Growing Soviet military power in the area tends to mute actual and potential differences among China, Japan, and the United States. It also sharply defines the inevitable stakes for each country should Soviet power remain unchecked.

While Japanese-Korean relations are stormy, a common view shared by the two countries and the United States is the need for peace and stability on the Korean peninsula. The highly strategic position of Korea has been underscored by the U.S. commitment to the defense of the ROK through the presence of U.S. military forces there. This military presence gives comfort and a sense of security to Japan and the ROK, but it also deeply involves the United States in the continuing political struggle between North and South Korea, a struggle watched carefully by the governments in Tokyo and Washington.

Koreans dislike Japanese and Japan barely conceals her arrogance toward Koreans, and especially toward the more than 600,000 Koreans living in alien status in Japan. These are core realities in the Japan-Korea relationship that make accommodation difficult and rapprochement nearly impossible. The legacy of Japanese repression and brutality during thirty-five years of its rule over Korea has left deep scars on Korean society and placed formidable obstacles in the way of a productive relationship.

ROK-Japan relations presently center principally on economic and trade issues, including Japanese support for South Korean industrial development, with occasional detours toward such sensitive problems as Japanese textbook accounts of Japan's military actions in World War II and statements of some Japanese leaders concerning Japan's occupation of Korea that are considered offensive by the ROK. In these political and trade skirmishes, the United States takes pains to distance itself from the two protagonists, concentrating its concerns mainly on the political and economic viability of the ROK and the military readiness of South Korean forces to deter military action from North Korea.

For Japan, Korea has always been linked to Japanese security. Because of this and Japan's economic and financial interests in South Korea, renewed hostilities on the Korean peninsula would have a greater impact on Japanese policy than anywhere else in Asia. With U.S. military bases in Japan acting as support elements for U.S. forces in the ROK, American, Japanese, and South Korean interests converge in common cause to maintain peace on the peninsula. Any actions from inside or outside Korea that disturb the present balance of power in the area are of deep concern to U.S.-Japan relations and to the South Koreans as well.

The troubled alliance is affected by many of the issues just described. To judge the capacity of the two countries to make the necessary accommodations and adjustments to meet new challenges, we must now contrast their societies, searching for those strengths and weaknesses that will ultimately determine the future of the U.S.-Japan relationship. Let us now turn to those differences.

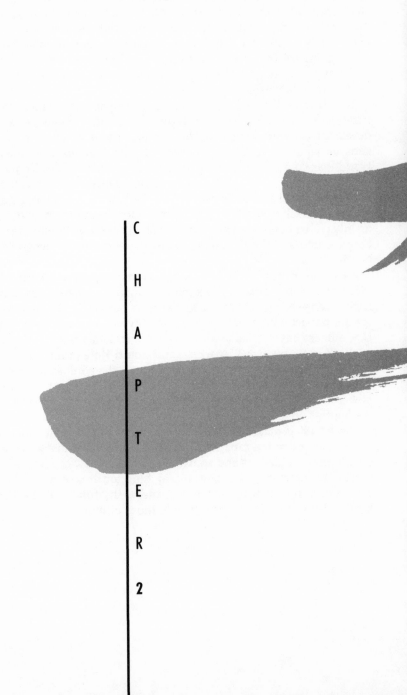

C
H
A
P
T
E
R

2

Contrasts between Japan and the United States have their roots in widely different cultural heritages. On February 11, 660 B.C., a date established by history and leavened with mythology, Japan's first emperor, Jimmu Tenno, ascended the throne of Yamato, the first Japanese "state." In 1940, the Japanese, in an outburst of nationalism symbolized by pageantry, commemorated the 2600th anniversary of the founding of their empire, ruled, as the official histories stated, by an unbroken line of emperors, from Jimmu to Hirohito. On July 4, 1976, the Americans marked the first 200 years of their existence as an independent nation, also with pageantry, including fireworks and tall ships.

Japan's isolation as an island nation, its lack of an indigenous written language, and its belief and pride in the divine origins of its leaders and people inculcated elements of character that have survived through the ages. Only from the early records of Chinese observers and from the mixture of mythology and glimmerings of history related in the first books of the eighth century A.D. do we begin to get a perception of an industrious, law-abiding people engaged in agriculture, weaving, and spinning, living close to na-

CONTRASTING SOCIETIES |

ture and worshipping the gods they believed created them and all things in heaven and on earth.

The Chinese ideographic system of writing had been introduced about A.D. 400 into a Japan which possessed no written language of its own. Many of the events described in the *Records of Ancient Matters* took place long before writing existed. An account of the shadowy transition from myth to history, the book traces the mythical beginnings of Japan and ends with a description of the death of the Empress Suiko in A.D. 628. Reciters are presumed to have passed on the narratives from one generation to another before the age of writing began. Known as the sacred book of the Shinto religion, the *Kojiki* and the *Nihongi*, or *Chronicles of Japan*, written in A.D. 637, were accepted as gospel, and schoolchildren in prewar Japan were taught their stories as history. The *Kojiki* was considered to be the embodiment of the "spirit of Japan."

According to ancient legend, seven generations of celestial spirits and five generations of terrestrial beings preceded Jimmu Tenno, who was a direct descendant of the Sun Goddess (Amaterasu-o-mikami), five generations removed. Consequently every Japanese emperor can claim a direct link in an unbroken line extending from the heavenly spirits who created the islands of Japan and favored them with their first human ruler.

Geology tells us that the Japanese islands were formed in the Pleistocene Age, more than two and a half million years ago. There must have been tremendous movements of mountains and rock structures, violent eruptions of volcanoes and shattering earthquakes, which changed the face of the land and its shores. Some forty volcanoes have been active in historic times, and the Japanese have become inured to the repeated earthquakes and fires that accompany them. In the past century the fires that so regularly devastated Tokyo, or Edo, as the capital was then named, were poetically called "the flowers of Edo." Until the near obliteration of Tokyo by fire bombing in 1945, the earthquake and fires of 1923 remained the benchmark of disaster in the Japanese memory. The Japanese people, in their respect and worship of the manifestations of nature as the principles of the Shinto religion, find in their beautiful and sacred Fuji, a mountain of volcanic origin long extinct, a symbol of their love of nature and of their country.

Humans inhabited the Japanese islands six to seven thousand years ago. Where they came from is still a matter of speculation. Most scholars believe the Northeast Asian strain is strongest, but wayfarers from the south and east also found their way through the centuries to shores in Japan. Another group, of a distinctly different racial type, is the Ainu, a primitive people whose origins are uncertain. At one time they were apparently spread throughout the Japanese islands but gradually receded to their last habitation, Hokkaido. In the eighth century frequent expeditions were undertaken to subjugate the Ainu, or "barbarians," as they were called. The first use of the title "shogun" in A.D. 794 was to designate the commander of a contingent assigned to fight the Ainu as *Sei-i-Tai-Shogun*, "Barbarian-Subduing-Generalissimo."

Long before the first Japanese books were written in the eighth century, Chinese historians had taken cognizance of the islands not far from their shores. There seems to have been travel back and forth among Chinese, Koreans, and Japanese from the first centuries of the Christian Era. The first mention of Japan in a Chinese book occurred in A.D. 57. In the third century a Chinese historian referred to Japan as Wa, using a Chinese character meaning "dwarf": "The people of Wa dwell in the middle of the ocean on mountainous islands. . . . They formerly comprised more than one hundred communities . . . thirty of their communities maintain intercourse with us through envoys and scribes."

The Japanese later combined the character for *Wa* with the character for great, pronouncing the resulting word "Yamato," which became the name of the first Japanese "state," an area surrounding the Nara plain and a short distance from Osaka, and founded by Jimmu Tenno supposedly in 660 B.C. In A.D. 737, the Japanese substituted for the *wa* signifying dwarf another ideograph, also pronounced *wa*, but with the felicitous meaning of "peace and harmony." *Yamato* thereafter became the symbol of Japan. Before and during World War II, it was used frequently, especially in the expression *Yamatodamashii* (Japanese spirit), which denoted the patriotic fervor intended to inspire the emperor's subjects. The use of the word "Yamato" diminished after the end of the war, and an alternative pronunciation for the same combination of characters, *Daiwa*, representing "Great Peace," came into more frequent usage.

Shinto, or the "Way of the Gods," grew in ancient times out of primitive man's affinity with nature, a belief that all things, animate and inanimate, partook of a spiritual essence that commanded respect and worship. The word *kami*, meaning deity, is applied to human beings, animals, natural phenomena such as thunder and lightning, plants, trees, seas, mountains, or—according to an eighteenth century scholar—anything whatsoever that was outside the ordinary, possessed superior power, or was awe-inspiring. Shrines were usually simple structures of unpainted wood and without images. Later influences from Buddhism and Confucianism affected the manifestations and organization of Shinto. In 1868, State Shinto was formed, supported by the government and devoted more and more to the glorification of the nation and of the emperor, who was declared by the Meiji constitution of 1889 to be "sacred and inviolable."

After World War II, occupation authorities regarded State Shinto as an insidious influence in Japan's march to militarism and aggression. It was abolished by order of General Douglas MacArthur, the Supreme Commander. The emperor, on January 1, 1946, publicly divested himself of sanctity in a radio address to the nation. Shinto, however, remains a non-governmental yet "national" religion. Japanese perform ablutions (washing and clapping of hands) before the shrines scattered throughout the country. The openings of new enterprises and the construction of new buildings are invariably blessed by Shinto priests and weddings are celebrated according to Shinto rites.

P resent day contrasts between Japan and the United States are enormous. As David MacEachron of the Japan Society of New York noted in a speech in Tokyo, the United States is a loose association of ethnic groups united by the deliberate and quite recent (in historical terms) adoption and continued acceptance of a constitution that determines the method for selection of government, sets limits thereon, and prescribes dispute-settling procedures.

Japan, to a much greater degree than any other large nation, is a creation of nature, a highly homogeneous people with traditions extending into prehistoric times. Compared to the people of other large nations, the Japanese see their country much more nearly as one great entity; they still have great trust in institutions of authority; and they have widely shared rules of behavior, which make unnecessary many of the written laws and regulations on which Americans depend.

Japan is an island nation and almost totally lacking in natural resources; the United States is continental and still rich in resources. Four of the fifty American states are each larger in area than all of the Japanese islands put together. Japan's climate is relatively mild and the rainfall abundant, although startling contrasts abound: The northernmost island of Hokkaido is snowy in winter and the southwestern island of Kyushu is warm and even semitropical in vegetation in some areas. Japan is a land of ever-present water—short, swift-running rivers, waterfalls, and volcanic lakes—and rain, sometimes propelled by the wind of typhoons that form in succession at certain times of the year, dramatically moving across sea and land to be recorded in vivid, satellite-beamed photographs watched avidly on millions of television sets.

Japanese speak a language that has no significant relationship to any other language in the world, a language with a particularly difficult written form. Americans, on the other hand, speak a world language and every American, apart from the American Indian, has to a greater or lesser degree a sense of kinship with one or more foreign countries or regions.

Americans would be uncomfortable if forced to live within the tight web that unites and controls Japanese through such institutions as the family, social convention, and (for many) large corporations or government agencies. Americans would probably not accept a government like that of Japan, which, at both national and local levels, is so intrusive in economic and private life.

Much of what explains Japan is integral to the most highly articulated large community in the world, where personal ambitions and mores are closely interrelated with the whole fabric of institutions, each tending to support the other. There is, of course, conflict and rivalry in Japan but, compared to America, Japan is extraordinarily harmonious.

The Japanese have a special attitude toward the human as a valuable resource to one's self and to one's community. Striving and achievement are deeply embedded in the Japanese psyche. The carp is admired in Japan because it battles its way upstream against the fierce current. The samurai ethic of selfless devotion to a leader or cause, fortified by intensive self-discipline and scornful of material advantage, is still a powerful influence. So also is the tea ceremony, a pervasive ethic with its teaching of elegant simplicity and harmonious quiet converse among friends.

Japan has a high regard for learning and the learned and is probably the only nation in the world whose supreme symbolic leader (the emperor) conducts an annual national poetry-writing contest. Although Japanese, like the rest of us, admire wealth, power and success, they also greatly admire the person who dedicates himself without reserve or regard for his own welfare to good causes. The Japanese are trained to be modest, and although this often conceals a fierce, understandable pride in Japan's achievements over the centuries, it also prepares the Japanese mind to learn from others. The Japanese consider their people to be their greatest resource. Because they comprise the largest homogeneous nation, with an acute sense of its own singularity, it is perhaps easier for the Japanese to view their whole population in this way.

The Japanese family is still a remarkably strong institution in spite of tremendous social change over the past four or five generations. Japanese children grow up in an intensely nurturing environment. At first the climate is extraordinarily permissive, but when at age four or five the child begins to learn discipline and the need to strive, the pressures begin to become intense. For example, the intensity of the pressure on the pre-university student has begun to produce concern. There is increasing evidence that teenagers' health is being adversely affected by the struggle to enter a prominent university.

By contrast, from its earliest beginnings, a strong, anti-intellectual streak has generally characterized the American ethos, alongside a belief in education as the path to Americanization and success. American society has always stressed the importance of individualism in the order of things. The powerful influence of the frontier strengthened this reverence for the individual. We treat our elected representatives, for example, with a mixture of respect for the power they temporarily wield and condescension for their presumed, or real, shortcomings in the face of often impossible tasks. The president and lesser officials often become the targets of hostility.

In Japan things are different. Although among younger Japanese even awareness of the emperor has greatly diminished, he is still a powerful moral influence. Centuries of profound respect for authority at all levels—father, professor, elders, employer, officials—grounded in Confucianism cannot be easily lost. Much of the Japanese strength depends upon the unusual skill with which they have harmonized the aspirations of individuals with national goals. An intense sense of Japanese uniqueness as a nation, in a world viewed with some suspicion and skepticism, is an element in helping to solidify the sense of community in Japan. The importance of strong family ties is another continuing influence. The handling of marriage demonstrates the significance the Japanese attach to the continuity of the family. While the arranged marriage is much less common in Japan today, the role of parents in seeking out suitable candidates for sons and daughters to marry is still strong. Japanese, by and large, are a contented people, savoring the strengths of their society and relishing their good fortune in becoming a powerful economic force in the world.

Japan has shifted from a deep belief in the divinity of the emperor and from a devotion to the creed of *bushido*, or the code of the warrior, to an unrelenting pursuit of economic advantage and the "good life." But certain convictions and views, as I have noted, remain consistent: Japan is unique; Japan mistrusts the "outsider"; Japan must export to survive; Japan must lead in showing less developed Asian nations the way to a better life; and Japan must preserve those special national characteristics that have propelled her to a leadership role in Asia—self-discipline, obedience to authority, harmony in personal relations, a dedication to the work ethic, an emphasis on the importance of education, the subordination of the individual to the group, and a reverence for family. Japanese insularity and the need to maintain social order in a nation of 120 million people crowded into four islands only 20 percent habitable have mandated certain social codes to insure that each individual and group has a place in society's web.

The United States, by contrast, has escaped the traumas that have afflicted Japan. In the past, we did, of course, fight Indians, carry out a revolution, brush with the British in 1812, engage in one of the cruelest civil wars ever fought, and use force to incorporate our Southwest. However, we have never suffered the devastation of a homeland as did our allies in World Wars I and II or occupation by foreign troops. We have never had to endure bombing of our cities as did our allies and our enemies in World War II. The end of the second

World War brought us victory and the unchallenged position as the greatest power on earth, although the Korean War and, far more so, the Vietnam War, dented our supreme confidence.

The size of the United States and its rich mineral and agricultural resources have made possible its world leadership in production. Japan, with 80 percent of its land area mountainous and its lack of the essential ingredients of an industrial state, notably oil, iron, coal, cotton, and other basic materials, is dependent on the outside world for necessities. The United States provides 80 percent of Japan's grain imports and 95 percent of its requirements for soybeans—an irreplaceable element in the Japanese diet, which in prewar days came from continental China. American farmers now supply annually over $7 billion worth of agricultural products to Japan, their leading customer.

The United States is a land of immigrants. A mixture of origins, races, religions, and character has formed our national psyche. Our nation used to be called a "melting pot" until the pride of ethnic origins began recently to assert itself. Japan, as we discussed earlier, is one of the most homogeneous nations on earth. Except for migrations in prehistoric times, probably from both north and south, the entry into the country of Koreans and Chinese in Japan's early centuries, and a brief infusion from Korea in the period before World War II, leaving some 600,000 Koreans in Japan, a purity of race and culture has persisted. This does not mean that Japan is devoid of minorities, although they are not present in large numbers.

Besides the Koreans, who are often treated as second-class citizens, remnants of the non-Japanese Ainu race still dwell on the island of Hokkaido. These are disappearing through absorption into the population by marriage. Another little talked of group forms the so-called *burakumin*, who, although racially identical to the Japanese, suffered discrimination for centuries as a class which engaged in the "unclean" slaughter and tanning of animals. Called the "invisible race," an estimated three million of these *burakumin* live principally in areas around Kyoto in western Japan.

Japan's origins and its homogeneity have engendered a pride of race and culture, a conscious "Japaneseness," giving strength to the people but at the same time creating barriers and irritations complicating Japan's relations with the rest of the world, especially with the United States.

The Japanese are finally beginning to succumb to the pressures of an increasingly interdependent world. These were first felt in the early 1860s, when Japan became aware of the outside world, especially of the actions of the Western imperialist powers in dismembering China, and of her own vulnerability. The opening of Japan to the West would reveal the inherent strengths of Japanese society—a national brawn that would draw admiration and create anxiety as Japan challenged the West. We now turn to an examination of the essence of this robust society.

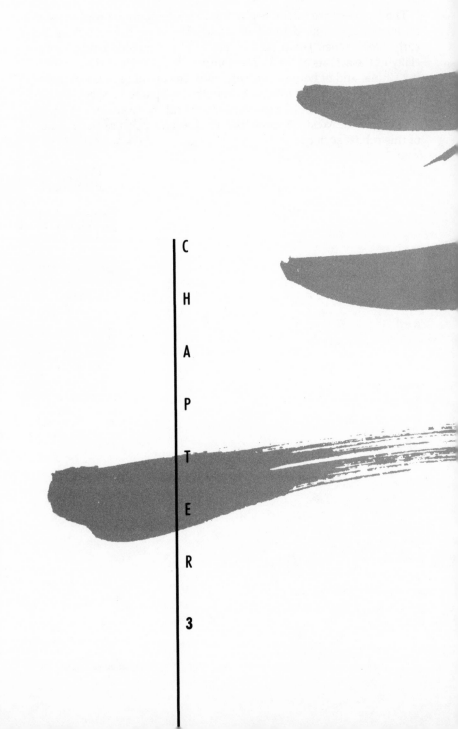

CHAPTER 3

Japan's strength derives from credos that have changed from time to time yet have an essence of continuity that gives its society the adaptability and resiliency to deal with natural and man-made adversity. These qualities played a critical role as Japan emerged from feudalism in the early 1860s. Other factors that exerted a fundamental influence on Japanese political and social development were China's culture, religion, and political system; internal military rule; early contacts with the West; and the Meiji Restoration, which was to underscore Japan's determination to discard an anachronistic feudalism and build a modern nation. We will first examine China's influence.

THE ESSENCE OF JAPANESE STRENGTH

The Chinese Legacy

Prince Shotoku, who served as "regent" during the reign of Empress Suiko (A.D. 592–628), and whose reign has been called one of the most remarkable periods in Japanese history, was steeped in the teachings of Confucianism and Buddhism. Buddhism is said to have come to Japan first through the presentation in 538 by the Korean state of Paekche to the Yamato court of a gilt-bronze image and Buddhist prayer scroll (*sutra*). Prince Shotoku became an ardent believer in Buddhism and did much to promote acceptance of the new religion, in spite of opposition by court rivals and practitioners of Shinto. It was soon declared the official religion of the country. This did not mean, of course, that the Japanese forsook their native beliefs.

The "Constitution" of 604, attributed to Shotoku, states in its first article that harmony is to be valued, and an avoidance of wanton opposition to be honored. Thus, by the seventh century, "harmony" (wa), which was to become a basic value of Japanese life, was clearly enunciated. Article 2 calls for reverence for the three Buddhist treasures: Buddha, the Law, and the Monastic Orders. Although often contradictory, Buddhism and Confucianism have coexisted happily throughout the years. Article 8 of Shotoku's "Constitution" propagates another ethical principle that has come down to modern times as representing Japanese diligence. It stipulates: "Let the ministers and functionaries attend the court early in the morning, and retire late. The business of the State does not admit remissness, and the whole day is hardly enough for its accomplishments."

A nineteenth century agrarian reformer, Ninomiya Sontoku, described the harmonious relationship existing among Shinto, Buddhism, and Confucianism, as the "pill" of the three religions. He described it thus: Shinto is the Way which provides for governing the country; and Buddhism is the Way which provides for governing one's mind. A friend asked the proportions of the prescription, to which Ninomiya replied: One spoon of Shinto; and a half spoon each of Confucianism and Buddhism. Someone divided a circle into half, representing Shinto, and two quarter segments representing Buddhism and Confucianism. Ninomiya rejected the diagram, commenting that medicine such as that did not exist. In a real pill all the ingredients are thoroughly blended so as to be indistinguishable. Otherwise it would taste bad in the mouth and feel bad in the stomach.

The most profound change wrought by the influence of China was the adoption of the Chinese ideographic writing system. The fact that the Japanese had never devised the written word and that their native language bore no relation whatsoever, either historically or linguistically, to Chinese, conveys an idea of the incredible difficulties created by imposing a totally foreign method of writing on the native spoken language of Japan. During several centuries Chinese was the written method of communication, largely carried on by scribes of Korean or Chinese origin and priests who had studied in China. Gradually Jap-

The infant Shotoku Taishi (Prince Shotoku) in mantra-chanting form. Japanese, Kamakura period, c. 1300. (Courtesy the Seattle Art Museum. Photo credit: Paul Macapia.)

anese influences began to assert themselves, indicated by changes in word order and usage that produced a mixture intelligible to those who knew both Chinese and Japanese. In the ninth century, according to tradition, Kobo Daishi, a priest who studied in China and founded the Shingon sect of Buddhism, invented a system called *kana*, in which simplified versions of Chinese characters were used as phonetic symbols. Previously only the complex Chinese ideographs could be used to indicate both Japanese and Chinese sounds as well as to represent meanings.

Gradually a form of Japanese writing developed as a combination of Chinese characters and the *kana* syllabaries, of which there were two, *kata kana* ("square" writing) and *hiragana* (cursive). Thus today to learn the national language every Japanese schoolchild must memorize a minimum of 1,945 officially designated Chinese characters, in addition to two sets of syllabaries with 48 signs each. The *kana* are now largely used as grammatical connectives and to spell out foreign words. Before World War II newspapers and other popular reading materials inserted tiny *kana* signs alongside the characters as a reader's aid to understanding the text. These, called *furigana*, are no longer used. In prewar Japanese schools, all students were required to learn, in addition to regular Japanese, *kanbun*, a kind of Chinese writing in which the word order had to be changed by the reader to make sense out of the text in Japanese.

Even some Japanese have recognized the handicap imposed upon them by their cumbersome language. In 1767 a Japanese scholar complained about how troublesome, evil, and turbulent the country of China was; to illustrate he referred to "the matter of their picture writing," complaining that "ever since Chinese writing was introduced we have mistakenly become enmeshed in it. In Holland, I understand, they use twenty-five letters. In this country there should be fifty."

Some eager reformers in General MacArthur's headquarters urged him to use his supreme power during the occupation to decree the writing of Japanese in Roman letters (*Romaji*), thus eradicating the punishing ideographs from the Japanese language. A stroke of the conqueror's pen appealed to them as a swift, clean way to remove an irksome problem, but fortunately such a destruction of Japan's cultural heritage was never seriously contemplated.

Not only did the Japanese adopt Buddhism, Confucianism, and language from China, but they modeled their political system along lines already in use in China. From a collection of tribes, the Japanese were able to institute a centralized government and to adopt the principle of authority by a single ruler. The Chinese concept of "Mandate of Heaven," in which a new emperor ascended the throne after the "Mandate" had been lost by the former monarch, was not implanted in Japan, where the principle of divine succession from the Sun Goddess had already been accepted. Forms of administrative practice were, however, borrowed from China. In the seventh and eighth centuries Japan adopted much from the then-flowering T'ang Era, including the systems of landholding as well as administration.

A capital was established, first at Nara and after seventy-five years, at Heian ("peace and tranquility"), the modern Kyoto. Both cities were designed in imitation of Chang An, the great Chinese capital of the T'ang Empire, and today Kyoto remains as one of the few Japanese cities with regularly laid out streets. The Nara and Heian periods endured for approximately 500 years, during which time the flowering of Japanese culture under Chinese and Buddhist influence developed. As has been said, "Art became religion, religion became art."

Military Rule

By A.D. 1100 a new military class had arisen and the *samurai* ("one who serves") became the heroes of Japanese history. The military capital was moved to Kamakura, although the emperor continued to live at his court in Kyoto. Feudalism and the institution of the *shogun*, the military leader and center of power, took their place alongside the growing influence of Buddhism. Zen Buddhism, first introduced from China in the seventh century, with its emphasis on discipline, concentration, and meditation and its lack of complicated scriptures, appealed especially to the military mind. It was hailed as "a special transmission outside the scripture; no dependence upon the written word; direct pointing at the soul of man; seeing one's nature and attaining Buddhahood."

In the thirteenth century the Mongols twice tried to invade Japan, but were driven away on both occasions by powerful typhoons, which earned the designation *kami-kaze*, meaning "divine wind" or "wind of the gods" (a term that was to reappear in World War II to honor the pilots who crashed their planes on American warships). The fourteenth and fifteenth centuries were a period of internal warfare. At one point there were rival northern and southern dynasties, only one of which was declared legitimate (claiming to have the sanction of the emperor) in order to carry on the unbroken line of the imperial succession. In the sixteenth century some progress toward order and unity began to appear, but it was through arms that the country was to be brought together. Three military leaders are given credit for consummating the unification and reconstruction of a sorely divided and chaotic Japan: Oda Nobunaga, Toyotomi Hideyoshi, and Tokugawa Ieyasu. A Japanese saying succinctly evaluates their accomplishments: Nobunaga piles the rice; Hideyoshi kneads the dough; Ieyasu eats the cake.

Opening to the West

Japan's first important meetings with the West occurred in the sixteenth century, although for many years Japanese seamen and pirates (*wako*) had explored and marauded in surrounding seas. In 1542 three Portuguese, driven north by a typhoon, landed on Tanegashima, an island off the southernmost tip of Kyushu beyond the strait of Osume. They were warmly received and were to be remembered in history for the firearms or arquebuses which they carried. The Japanese had never seen a firearm before and for many centuries the name for musket in Japanese was *tanegashima*.

In 1549 Francis Xavier, a Jesuit missionary, and several companions landed at Kagoshima and began to preach, without interference from the Japanese. Nobunaga treated the Christian missionaries well, partly because he was engaged in bitter feuds with the Buddhists. Hideyoshi, who succeeded Nobunaga after the latter's assassination, continued to tolerate missionaries, and by 1582 they claimed to have made 150,000 converts. One can imagine the problem in propagating a new religion through the transmission of foreign abstract ideas in a totally alien language. Serious disagreement developed, for example, over the proper translation of the word "God." *Kami*, as we have seen, meant spirits in all of nature and was far from the Christian concept of one god. There was no other choice, however, and Kami is the Christian god.

Without warning, Hideyoshi in 1587 banned the missionaries, probably out of fear that they were becoming too influential among his vassals. After ten years of somewhat lax enforcement he reimposed the ban with a vengeance, crucifying a number of Spanish Franciscans, Portuguese Jesuits, and Japanese Christians. It was not until 1640, however, that, having made illegal the departure of any foreign missionaries from the country, the Tokugawa government shut the door to all Europeans, permitting some trade with Chinese and leaving only a small group of Dutchmen on the tiny island of Deshima, off Nagasaki. Thus began Japan's "closed period," which was to last more than two hundred years.

Hideyoshi had dreams of conquest and even envisaged establishing his capital at Peking, thus uniting his then known world of China, Korea, and Japan. On July 5, 1587, he wrote to his wife, "I have sent fast ships in order to urge even Korea to pay homage to the Emperor of Japan, stating that, if it does not, I shall conquer it next year. I shall take even China in hand, and have control of it during my lifetime; since China has become disdainful of Japan, the work will be the more exhausting." Hideyoshi engineered two expeditions to Korea, threatened the Ming empire in China and thus hastened its end, but achieved no victories. He died in 1598. The presence of thousands of Japanese in Korea and their return with war booty contributed significantly to posterity by an added infusion of continental culture.

Hideyoshi, although renowned largely for his military exploits, has been regarded by some historians as a major contributor to the modernization of Japan. Among his notable domestic reforms were the separation of the samurai from the peasantry and their establishment as a new urban class; a land survey, with the registration of all agricultural land; and, finally, a so-called "sword hunt," in which he confiscated the weapons of all Japanese except those of the samurai class. This act of disarmament had a profound effect, instilling a national tradition that to this day makes the possession of weapons by the Japanese citizenry an almost unheard of phenomenon.

Tokugawa Ieyasu, the third in the line of unifiers of Japan, was designated shogun in 1603. He is the *Shogun* made famous by the popular but historically distorted novel of that name. The administration of the Tokugawa shogunate, called *Bakufu*, which means "tent government," to suggest the field headquarters of an army, was established at a new capital, Edo, on the Kanto plain. The emperor and his court remained at Kyoto. The domain, which thanks to the conquests of Hideyoshi and Ieyasu now comprised the whole country, was divided into realms, or *han*, each under the control of a lord, or *daimyo*, and numbering some 295 in the early Tokugawa period. Although each *daimyo* enjoyed a large degree of autonomy, he was subject to control by the *Bakufu*, one major method being the system of *sankin kotai* ("attendance by turn"), which required the *daimyo* and their retinues of retainers to reside alternately in their domain and in the capital, leaving wives and children as hostages in Yedo. The periods of residence varied but were usually one year in each place.

Tokugawa Japan was an agricultural economy. Of an estimated population of thirty million, some twenty-four million were farmers. Wealth was measured in units of rice, one *koko* being equivalent to about five bushels. A strict hierarchy of classes was maintained, with farmers fourth in rank—after nobles, samurai, and artisans; merchants and actors were at the bottom of the scale. The importance of the farmers was recognized, yet their sufferings were great. An early nineteenth-century writer described their lot: "The farmers, it is stated, till the soil with the labor of their bodies. . . . In summer they are scorched by the sun, suffering together with the horses and cattle; while in winter they endure the hardships of cold. The products of their labors are heavily taxed . . . and, producing the cereals and necessities of the country, they are in truth, those who have contracted for the work of all. They are the foundation of the state, the treasures of the world." There were more than 1000 peasant uprisings during the 250 years of the Tokugawa period.

The Meiji Restoration

The Meiji Restoration of 1868 meant literally that Emperor Meiji, who had his court in Kyoto and had been "persuaded" to delegate power to his regent, the Tokugawa shogun, was restored to primacy as the embodiment of the state by rebellious clans. After the overthrow of the Tokugawa shogunate, Emperor Meiji moved his court to Tokyo, known in 1868 as Edo, and a national government was established. The mainsprings of the Meiji Restoration were the breakdown of the Tokugawa system and pressure from without. The relative importance of these two factors is still being debated by scholars, especially the question of whether Japan would have evolved in the direction of modernization had there been no knock on the door. Certainly the combination of the two pressures brought about a climax of change that could not otherwise have occurred so quickly. As Sir George Sansom concludes in his book, *The Western World and Japan* (1950), "Every force but conservatism was pressing from within at the closed doors: so that when a summons came from without they were flung wide open, and all these imprisoned energies were released."

Erosion of the Tokugawa administration had been proceeding for many years, speeded up in the early 1800s by economic and financial difficulties. Famines and peasant uprisings were causing frequent disruptions, and although one reformer after another had proposed changes, the shogun had shown great ineptitude in dealing with mounting problems. Dissatisfactions were affecting all classes: The nobles wanted industry and trade to develop the resources of their domains; the samurai wanted opportunities to use their talents, whether as soldiers or officials; the merchants wanted to break the monopolies of the guilds; the scholars wanted to draw knowledge from new springs; and the peasants and townsmen wanted a little freedom from taxes and tyranny.

For the increasingly nervous Japanese, the question became one of how to respond to these accumulating initiatives. As a sidelight on the frustrations of those tense days, Fukuzawa Yukichi, a young samurai who had learned Dutch in Osaka and came to Edo in 1853, discovered to his dismay when he later visited Yokohama that signs were in English, foreign seamen were speaking English, and the Dutch he had so painfully mastered was not an international language. To communicate with foreigners he must learn yet another tongue. Discouraged as he was, he mastered English and became one of the best and most influential of teachers, speakers, and writers. He inspired bright young intellectuals to push forward the inevitable modernization of his country, and became the founder of the present Keio University in Tokyo.

Like the founding fathers who drew up the Constitution of the United States, these samurai who indefatigably built the new order in the name of Emperor Meiji were young men averaging slightly over thirty years of age in 1868. They had led the rebellion against the Tokugawa shogun, had a high level of education and training, had experience in local government service, and were mostly from southwestern Japan, from the clans in Kyushu, Shikoku, and southwestern Honshu—Satsuma, Choshu, Hizen, and Tosa. Many had followed military careers and were therefore "men of action"; several had already been abroad and had some association with foreigners. Their objectives were to secure the state and to strengthen it against the West. They had begun to think of a more powerful government over and above the *han*, which were to become prefectures with little power.

There were, of course, differences among the creators of the new Japan: Some followed the slogan *Sonno Joi* (Revere the Emperor, Expel the Barbarians); others, *Fukko* (Return to the Past); but most important were the leaders who believed fervently in *Fukoku Kyohei* (Prosperous

Country, Strong Military). This last became the guiding principle of Japan and was still very much the ambition of the militarists who gained control of the nation in the 1930s.

The basic documents of the Restoration illustrate the tug between traditionalism and modernization. The Charter Oath, signed by the emperor in April 1868, representing the progressive side of the Restoration, provided that deliberative assemblies should be set up; declared unity of all classes, high and low; proclaimed liberties for the common people; enjoined the breaking of evil customs of the past and the seeking of knowledge throughout the world. The Imperial Rescript on Education (October 30, 1890), enshrined in every school in the country, stressed the sacred nature of the emperor, calling for the guarding and maintenance of "the prosperity of Our Imperial Throne coequal with heaven and earth," and ordered that "The Way here set forth is indeed teaching bequeathed by Our Imperial Ancestors, to be observed alike by Their Descendants and the subjects, infallible for all ages and true in all places."

The constitution of 1889, while establishing a limited parliamentary system of two houses, a house of representatives and a house of peers, declared the emperor to be sacred and sovereign and included a "bill of rights," which specified that each asserted "right" existed only "according to law," which meant that a mere act of the Diet, as the parliament was to be called, could abrogate the right. The constitution, by endowing the emperor with the power of supreme command over the army and navy, in fact gave ministers of the army and navy direct access to the throne. In 1900 an imperial ordinance stipulated that army and navy ministers must be active military officers. Thus, the army and navy, by refusing to nominate an active duty officer as army or navy minister, made it impossible for a prime minister to form a government.

A debatable question is whether the Meiji Restoration set Japan on a track which would inevitably lead to World War II. Certainly the sense of weakness and futility vis-a-vis the West deeply determined Japanese leaders to build defenses so that the nation might take a respectable place among the nations of the world. The Meiji founders, following the example of Western imperialists before them, determined that the road to needed raw materials lay through colonies, and the road to colonies could be opened only through arms. In an expanding and increasingly competitive trading world, Japan saw her destiny first in her neighbor China. Korea lay in the way, as it had for Hideyoshi in the sixteenth century. Japan fought a war with China in 1894–1895, sparked by Korea, and a war with Russia in 1904, to prevent Russian hegemony over Korea. Victory in these wars gave Japan great confidence and its military leaders great prestige. Japan also saw that military power added significantly to her international prestige and to her ability to get her own way in her march toward "big power" status. The momentum generated by these early military victories moved Japan inexorably toward expansion of her sphere of influence in the Western Pacific and ultimate confrontation with the United States.

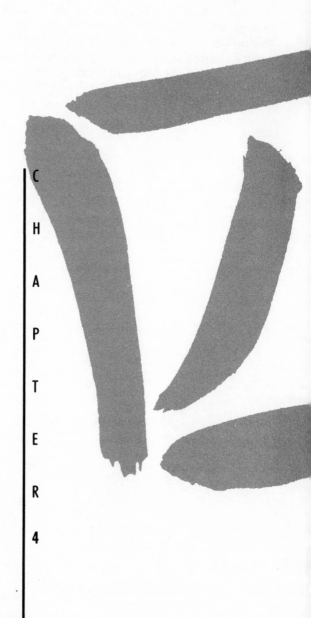

C
H
A
P
T
E
R

4

From 1790 until the date of Commodore Matthew Perry's first arrival in Japan in 1853, twenty-seven American ships visited Japan, three of them warships. Two unsuccessful efforts were made by Americans to open Japan to foreign trade: In 1832 a sea captain named Edmund Roberts was empowered by the United States government to negotiate treaties in Asia, including Japan, but he died en route to his destination. In 1846, after changes of personnel due to death and illness, Commodore James Biddle, chief of the East India squadron, set out under orders in two warships, the *Columbus* and the *Vincesses*, to arrive off Uraga, near present Tokyo Bay, on July 20. After several days of obviously animated discussion between Japanese authorities in Uraga and at Yedo, the capital, and with Biddle, the official answer supplied to him denied the request for trade, ordered the two ships to leave as soon as possible, and warned that it would be useless to come again, no matter how often. The warships departed on July 29.

The third American warship, the sixteen-gun sloop *Preble*, was dispatched to Nagasaki to rescue fifteen American seamen who had deserted their ship and were being confined in Nagasaki. Although the Japanese insisted that the American seamen should depart on a Dutch vessel, they finally relented and the seamen were repatriated on the *Preble* on April 27, 1849, with this warning to be communicated to the captain: "In future, these boats must never again come to fish in neighboring waters. Deliver these men to the captain of the American ship with this warning."

Other efforts were made to break down Japan's exclusionist policy before the Perry mission. On October 18, 1792, a Russian emissary, Lt. Adam Laxman, brought two Japanese castaways to Nemuro in Hokkaido and asked for an opening of trade relations. After a six-month wait for word to come from the bakufu in Edo, the request was refused. A second Russian attempt was made in October 1804 by a Russian ambassador, Count Nikolai Petrovich Rezanov, who arrived at Nagasaki in the warship *Nadezhda*. The Japanese replied on April 5 of the following year, refusing to receive the ambassador and demanding the departure of the ship. The Dutch themselves made a plea for broadened intercourse through the visit of a Dutch warship at Nagasaki, bearing a letter from King William II of Holland. The warship departed on November 27, and in July of the following year the bakufu replied, refusing to accede to the King's requests.

The Perry Expedition

The admission of California as a state of the Union in 1850 at the end of the Mexican War, the discovery of gold, and the growing importance of coal to fuel the newly invented steamships all contributed to the consciousness of the United States as a "Pacific" power. The pressure to open relations with Japan increased, spurred also by competition, especially from the Russians. In his report to Congress of his expedition in 1852–1853 to the China Sea and Japan, Perry likens the position of the United States, between two oceans, to the "Middle Kingdom," replacing the China of old.

Perry's squadron of four ships arrived in Tokyo Bay on the morning of July 8, 1853. American intentions to attempt to open trade with Japan had been publicly announced a year in advance. The Dutch in 1852 were ordered by the Japanese government to negotiate with the chief at Deshima "about the means the latter should indicate in order to preserve Japan against the dangers that threatened her." Without informing the United States, which had addressed a note to the Netherlands in July 1852 asking for cooperation in the Perry enterprise, the

Dutch king had transmitted a draft treaty intended to "mitigate the severe laws against foreigners." The treaty had provided for an open port only at Nagasaki, where the Dutch had of course been long established.

A Russian squadron appeared at Nagasaki on August 22, 1853, remained until November, and made several arrivals and departures, fruitlessly seeking interviews, until April 26, 1854. Perry did not like the Russians and believed that the Japanese distrusted them. He refused to take as interpreter on the expedition probably the best informed foreigner in Japan, who had spent much time in Nagasaki and Edo, Baron Philip Franz von Siebold, an Austrian scientist and physician working with the Dutch. Von Siebold had been accused of purloining secret documents and had been deported from Japan, according to Perry's account, under the charge of acting as a Russian spy. The commodore's feelings about Russia were eloquently expressed in a paper which he read in New York, after his return from Asia, to the American Geographical and Statistical Society on March 6, 1856:

> It seems to me that the people of America will, in some form or other, extend their dominion and their power, until they shall have placed the Saxon race upon the eastern shore of Asia. And I think too that eastward and southward will her great rival in future aggrandizement (Russia) stretch forth her power and thus the Saxon and the Cossack will meet. Will it be in friendship? I fear not! The antagonistic exponents of freedom and absolutism must thus meet at last, and then will be fought the mighty battle. . . . On its issue will depend the freedom or the slavery of the world. . . . I think I see in the distance the giants that are growing up for that fierce and final encounter; in the progress of events that battle must sooner or later be fought.

Perry embarked on his enterprise well prepared; he had amassed the information available, both official and private and including some forty books then in existence. He took with him instructions from the State Department and from the Navy Department, both dated November 1852, and a letter from President Millard Fillmore to the Emperor of Japan. From his flagship the *Susquehanna* Perry wrote a letter addressed to the emperor dated July 7, 1853, asking for an audience to present the president's letter. (Franklin Pierce had meanwhile become president on March 4, 1853.) After much discussion, during which Perry maintained a calculated aloofness, refusing to be seen during any of the pourparlers on shipboard, a compromise was reached whereby Perry would go ashore with his retinue and deliver both the original of the president's letter and a copy. This was accomplished, with much pomp and ceremony, on July 14. Expecting that an answer would be long in coming, Perry decided to leave Japan at once, returning for the reply the following spring. On February 25, 1854, the squadron was back at anchor off Kanagawa, and on March 31 the treaty was signed, opening Japan's closed door.

Diplomatic Overtures

The treaty Perry had signed provided that the United States would be permitted to appoint consuls or agents to reside in Shimoda "at any time after the expiration of eighteen months from the date of the signing of this treaty; provided that either of the two governments deems such arrangements necessary." Townsend Harris, appointed the first consul, arrived in Shimoda on August 21, 1856. He was anxious to take up his duties as soon as possible and the Japanese were just as anxious to delay the proceedings, realizing that they were creating precedents. Finally, and after sometimes heated negotiations, Harris was received in audience at Yedo by the shogun on December 7, 1856.

Townsend Harris accomplished two important tasks during his sojourn in Japan. The first was the negotiation and conclusion of the "Convention of Shimoda" on June 17, 1857, which extended somewhat the rights and privileges of Americans in Japan. According to Harris's diary, it took nine days just to settle the *wording* of the articles, largely because the Dutch of the Japanese interpreters was that which ship captains had used some two hundred and fifty years before. His mood is well understood when he writes to the secretary of state on June 18 that he has not received any dispatches from the department since he left the United States in October 1855. He laments to his diary on June 23 that he has been out of flour, bread, butter, lard, bacon, hams, sweet oil, and in fact out of every kind of foreign supply for more than two months. He adds: "My health is miserable, my appetite is gone, and I am so shrunk away that I look as though a 'Vice-Consul had been cut out of me.'"

The consul's second and more important duty was the negotiation of a Treaty of Amity and Commerce between the United States and Japan, concluded at Yedo on July 29, 1858, and ratified by President Buchanan on April 12, 1860. The exchange of ratifications of the commercial treaty was carried out in Washington on May 22, 1860, on the occasion of the visit to the United States of the first Japanese embassy representatives sent by the Tokugawa Shogunate.

The "embassy" of 1860 consisted of seventy-two persons and traveled on the U.S. frigate *Powhatan*, sent to Japan for the purpose. The *Powhatan* was escorted by a Japanese ship, the *Kanrin Maru*, a gift from the Dutch but operated by Japanese officers and crew. At the request of the Japanese, Lieutenant Brooke, an experienced naval officer, accompanied the *Kanin Maru* on her voyage to San Francisco to assist the Japanese navigators. This ship was the first Japanese steamer ever to cross the Pacific. The Japanese were proud of this unprecedented achievement, although some later historians have concluded that if it had not been for the presence of Lieutenant Brooke, the *Kanin Maru* might not have achieved such a successful crossing.

The welcome given the Japanese in Washington was tumultuous. It was described by a correspondent for the *New York Illustrated News*:

> The excitement in Washington, consequent upon the arrival of the Japanese Embassy, far exceeds anything which the old Myth, known by the name of 'Oldest Inhabitant,' has within the records of his remembrances. We have seen many notable sights in our time; many magnificent gatherings and processions of the great American people, on many various occasions—but the reception of the Embassy on their landing in this city was the grandest spectacle which one great nation has ever, perhaps, presented to the Envoys and Ambassadors of another. Certainly it was the grandest spectacle which we have ever beheld, and its parallel, if it is to be found anywhere, must be sought for in antique trophies—*bellorum exuviae* as Juvenal has it, and was received with wild shouts and acclamation, and the mighty roar of Rome.

Harper's Weekly of August 1860 expressed a more sober judgment: that the Japanese "seemed to have an aptitude for acquiring the civilization of the West to which no other oriental race can claim."

A more imposing mission, in terms of its personnel, was sent to the United States and Europe by Emperor Meiji's order in January 1872. The head of the "embassy" was Iwakura Tomomi, vice president of the Council of State, who was accompanied by some of the outstanding leaders of the Meiji Restoration, forty-nine in all. Besides these dignitaries there were five young ladies—the first women ever sent overseas for education—and fifty-three young men and servants. Iwakura had considered seeking revision of the treaty but decided in the end to postpone this effort. The influence of the mission's visit on subsequent developments in Japan was significant; members probed untiringly into every phase of Western society, especially industry, education, and government. Of the five Japanese girls, one studied at Vassar College and later married Prince and Field Marshal Oyama Iwao, hero of the Russo-Japanese War; another, the youngest at eight years of age, Tsuda Ume, pursued facilities for women's education, and after ten years in the United States returned to Japan where she later founded an institute for girls in Tokyo, which became the present Tsuda College for Women, the best and most famous women's college in Japan today.

These auspicious starts brought Japan closer to the United States than to any other foreign country. Numerous American teachers and missionaries sojourned in Japan, bringing to bear a lasting influence on education and on the process of westernization, already proceeding at a rapid pace. Meanwhile, the Meiji goal of *fukoku kyohei* ("rich country, big military") was being pursued with the relentless determination that later brought both hatred and admiration to the country. China was defeated and Taiwan annexed in 1895; Japan entered the world of foreign powers by signing the Anglo-Japanese Alliance in 1902; and in a confrontation with Russia over Korea, defeated the Russians in 1905. By 1897, Japan's arms budget had increased five times over annual military expenditures before the Sino-Japanese War.

The United States was observing Japan's reach for greater prestige and influence through diplomatic and military means with growing apprehension. America's acquisition of the Philippines, fulfilling, as some Washington commentators said, "our Manifest Destiny," introduced a new element into U.S. foreign policy—protecting the Philippines and our other interests in the area. The United States saw an ambitious and unrestrained Japan as a potential threat to these interests. Japan saw the United States as a competitor for power and influence in the Pacific.

Relations Sour

Japanese-American relations had begun to sour as the new century began. The United States was taking an increasing interest in Pacific affairs, thereby posing to Japanese eyes a threat to Japan's interests in the region. Washington annexed Hawaii in 1897 and the Western Samoan islands in 1899; and the Spanish-American War of 1898 established the Philippine Islands as part of the United States. Secretary of State John Hay in 1899 and 1900 was proclaiming the "Open Door" policy for China, which clashed with Japan's developing expansionist policies and concepts of a "special interest" in China. Hay had not secured anything approaching an international guarantee of the open door or the "territorial and administrative entity" of China. He had merely oriented American policy toward a more active participation in Far Eastern politics in support of those principles. This emphasis on "principles" and its clash with Japanese policy were to color U.S.-Japan relations up until the outbreak of war in December 1941.

Another cause of growing U.S.-Japan alienation, as we have seen, was Japan's expanding military power through triumphs achieved in victories over China and Russia and the acquisition of Taiwan in 1895 and of Korea in 1910. Japan developed a self-image as the leading military power in East Asia, with the United States as the obstacle.

A third cause, with serious implications for American domestic politics, was the treatment of Japanese in the United States. Racism was fanned by the growing presence of Japanese. By 1897 they were already the largest ethnic group in the Hawaiian Islands, and by 1900 those in the entire United States numbered two-thirds of all Japanese living abroad. In 1894 West Coast Japanese were denied citizenship on the basis of race. In 1913 a California law prohibited Japanese from owning land since they were ineligible for citizenship. In 1922 and 1923 the Supreme Court confirmed that Japanese could not become citizens and upheld the alien land laws of California and other states. The Immigration Law of 1924, called the Exclusion Act, denied entry into the United States to "aliens ineligible for citizenship," which em-

braced all Orientals but particularly struck the Japanese, whose ambassador had warned in advance that passage of the law would have
"grave consequences" for the otherwise mutually advantageous relations between Japan and the United States. In wartime (December
1943) Congress removed the exclusion provisions against Chinese,
but it was not until the Immigration Act of 1952 that Japanese were
placed on the quota basis applicable to all nationalities.

While Japanese-American relations continued to deteriorate, efforts
were being made by organizations in both the United States and Japan
to create better understanding between the two countries. A Japan
Society was organized in New York in 1907 and a comparable America-Japan Society was established in Tokyo. These organizations
worked tirelessly to promote understanding and friendship, and, except for the hiatus of the war years, have continued to do so until the
present day.

The United States was increasingly ambivalent in its policy toward
Japan as the two nations entered the decade of the 1930s. China had
always been the crux of the conflict and remained so until the end.
The United States, although repeatedly championing the "independence and territorial integrity" of China, at the same time recognized
Japan's "special position" in Manchuria and Japan's "special interests" in China. This ambivalence was mainly the result of concern for
protection of U.S. interests in China and a reluctance to engage Japan
in a military confrontation there. Later, however, after Japan's invasion
of Manchuria in 1931, Secretary of State Stimson proclaimed his "non-
recognition doctrine" that henceforth the United States would not recognize gains made or changes accomplished as a result of the employment of military force. In 1933 President Franklin D. Roosevelt
placed the responsibility on Japan for the takeover of Manchuria.
After the creation by Japan of the state of "Manchukuo" in February
1932, Japan's insistence on her "special responsibility" for the maintenance of peace in East Asia became more strident.

For all its proclamations of the principles of the territorial integrity
and independence of China, the United States did not suggest that
it would go to war to defend those principles. Although the navies
of both countries regarded their counterparts as "hypothetical enemies" and all naval training was directed toward an eventual Japanese-American war, neither side officially threatened war. In a campaign speech in Boston in October 1940, President Roosevelt

resoundingly declared: "I have said this before, but I shall say it again, and again and again. Your boys are not going to be sent into any foreign wars."

The Shadow of War

The mood of a historical period is not communicated in the dry documents of diplomacy. Those of us who lived in Tokyo in the prewar years constantly considered the possibility of war between Japan and the United States but clung to the belief that it could be prevented. We watched the efforts on the home front to sustain a war in China in which the imperial armies were becoming "bogged down." We disparaged the Japanese. Their overblown slogans seemed ridiculous: "Eight Corners of the Universe under One Roof," "The Holy War," "A Hundred Million People with One Heart," "The New Order in East Asia," and "The Co-Prosperity Sphere in East Asia." The evidence of food, fuel, and clothing shortages was all around us. Disintegrating "staple fiber" (*sufu*) supplanted cotton cloth. Necessities were rationed. When gasoline became unavailable for private automobiles, they were converted into wood-burners. Taxi drivers would stop their cars, go to the back, and stoke the fire in the compartment where the trunk had been.

The Datsun automobile was regarded by most foreigners as a joke, as was Suntory whiskey. Air raid drills (*boku-enshu*), with frantic positioning of black curtains over windows at the sound of sirens, were pathetic gestures to protect flammable wooden houses. Early morning regimented calisthenics in the streets, to blaring radio instructions, looked like brave but ineffectual attempts to build the national physique. All the while, flag-waving send-offs of sons and brothers to war were daily occurrences.

These observations confirmed, if confirmation were needed, the "realities" of Japan's vulnerability and total dependence on the outside world for essential raw materials. And for Japan of the 1930s, military power was the accepted way to build economic power. While to us a Japanese war against the "invincible" United States appeared preposterous, the leaders of the Empire, dedicated to policies of expanding Japan's influence in Asia since the Meiji period, were ready, if faced with no other perceived alternative, to go to war.

Joseph C. Grew, American ambassador in Japan from 1932 to 1941, saw during those years a developing Japanese-American rift over "principles" and "realities." In 1900 Americans had proclaimed the Open Door in China, and in 1922 the Nine Power Treaty had bound the United States to "respect" (but not "defend") the sovereignty, independence, and territorial and administrative integrity of China. We never committed ourselves to go to war in support of these principles. Henry L. Stimson, secretary of state in 1932, tried in vain to get British support to cite Japan as a violator of this treaty after the Manchurian "incident" (*jiken*) of September 1931. This incident, designed to solidify Japanese influence and rights in Manchuria, was an early harbinger of difficulties for Sino-Japanese relations. The Japanese government was determined to maintain the rights it had acquired in Manchuria because of what Japan considered the economic indispensability of Manchuria to the well-being and even to the continued existence of Japan. Japan emphasized the essentiality of Manchurian coal, iron, and other resources for Japanese industrialization.

Growing Chinese nationalism confronted Japanese Manchurian policy, and tensions between the two countries grew until an explosion occurred in 1937, with Japan expanding her sphere of influence by moving against Chinese Nationalist military forces in North China. Thus began the prolonged Sino-Japanese War that was ultimately to lead Japan to Pearl Harbor and war with the United States. Reacting to Japan's invasion of North China, President Roosevelt proposed a "quarantine" of aggressors, meaning principally Japan. The public outcry in the United States was deafening, with calls for the impeachment of the president and organized campaigns to "keep the U.S. out of war!" In Tokyo, Ambassador Grew exclaimed to the administrative officer who handed him the telegram summarizing the "quarantine" speech: "There goes everything I have tried to accomplish in my entire mission to Japan." Even Cordell Hull, Secretary of State, thought "quarantine" too drastic a word, believing that Americans had to be led gradually out of their isolationist mood.

By 1939 war had spread in China and anti-Japanese feeling was growing in the United States. Notice to terminate the American commercial treaty with Japan was greeted with public approval. Grew, on home leave, was astonished at the strength of sentiment for a trade embargo and warned the State Department and his fellow citizens that a policy of sanctions could lead to war. Back in Japan, he tried to explain to the Japanese the feelings of Americans over the Empire's "sacred" war in China. In his "straight from the horse's mouth" speech, delivered to the America-Japan Society in Tokyo on October 19, he admonished his listeners: "The American people have good reason to believe that an effort is being made to establish control, in Japan's own interest, of large areas on the continent of Asia and to impose upon those areas a system of closed economy." Grew concluded that Japanese leaders paid attention to his speech and were sobered by it.

Widening divergencies were developing between those in charge of East Asian affairs at the State Department and Grew's embassy in Tokyo during 1939 and 1940. The ambassador's New England conscience supported wholeheartedly the "principles" on which our policy stood but he also recognized the "realities" which guided Japan: strategic protection against Soviet attack, economic security through control of raw materials in China, and eradication of anti-Japanese and communist activities and propaganda in China. He saw two courses for American policy: one, "intransigence," including refusal to negotiate a new treaty of commerce and the imposition of an embargo; the other, which he recommended, was a willingness to discuss a new treaty and postpone an embargo.

In the process, the American side would of course urge observance of the Nine-Power Treaty of 1922, which had attempted to resolve conflicting interests in the Pacific area, especially those involving China, Siberia, and the Pacific mandated islands, and respect for American rights in China. Grew believed that Japan's determination to win influence in China would not be deterred by the termination of the treaty or by an embargo. On the contrary, the Japanese samurai spirit of stoicism and determination would be hardened. War could result but not renunciation of the nation's aims, which, from the time of Meiji, had been "prosperity and military strength" (*fukoku kyohei*), to which had been added a "hegemonial position in East Asia."

Stanley K. Hornbeck, whose only experience in Asia had been a teaching stint in China, was the senior adviser on Far Eastern matters to Secretary of State Hull. Hornbeck found Grew's arguments unpersuasive and red-pencilled his dispatches and diaries with bold dissent. Hornbeck's prescribed method was to "freeze out" the Japanese, to "put the screws on." He visualized Grew and his staff as subject to the stultifying atmosphere of Tokyo, in which well-meaning Japanese "friends" told them what they wanted to hear.

The year 1940 brought to Japan an intensification of "spiritual mobilization," the abolition of political parties and their replacement by the military-dominated Imperial Rule Assistance Association. On September 12, Grew shifted his position and for the first time recommended the gradual, progressive application of measures against Japan. He warned that a "drastic" embargo would likely encounter retaliation that might take the form of a "sudden stroke" by the military, and therefore counseled Washington to face squarely the consequences of whatever action it might take.

Meanwhile the Japanese government, after lengthy deliberations among army, navy, and political leaders over the value of joining in a military pact with the Axis, concluded on September 27, 1940, that it was in Japan's interest to join with Nazi Germany and Fascist Italy in a pact—the Tripartite Pact—that called for each party to assist the others with all political, economic, and military means if one of the parties were attacked by a country not presently involved in the European war or in the Sino-Japanese conflict.

Grew was crushed by Japan's adherence to the Axis; Admiral Yonai Mitsumasa, the previous prime minister, had assured him that this would not happen. He confided to his diary that a typhoon could hardly have more effectively demolished the foundation of Japanese-American relations. The Japanese recognized the seriousness of the step. In the Imperial Conference which took the decision, the president of the Privy Council pleaded only for time: "Even though a Japanese-American clash may be unavoidable in the end, I hope that sufficient care will be exercised to make sure that it will not come in the near future."

Three basic issues separated the two sides: Japan's adherence to the Axis pact, the principle of equal commercial opportunity, and Japanese troops in China. By the latter part of 1941 the Japanese were already disillusioned by their German ally. Joining the Axis had not been a profitable move; they had received no help from Hitler or Mussolini. To denounce the Axis publicly would have been difficult, but Japanese negotiators had assured their American counterparts that the Tripartite Pact would automatically become a dead letter if a Japanese-American agreement were achieved. The problem of equal commercial opportunity was not insoluble. The presence of Japanese forces in China and Indochina was the sticking point. The army was overcommitted on the continent and had not succeeded in destroying the Nationalist government of China.

Japan's leaders were ready to effect partial withdrawal from both Indochina and mainland China. They could not, however, accept the demand for a total evacuation of both countries, probably including Manchuria, which was contained in the note delivered to Ambassador Nomura on November 26 and which Japan regarded as an ultimatum. A nation which, although mired in fruitless combat, had not been defeated, could not at once abandon an enterprise upon which so many years of sacrifice had been expended. Americans were later, in Vietnam, to suffer at firsthand the excruciating experience of withdrawing from a prolonged war. In 1941 our obsession with China as a "Great Power" and an ally, and with the Chinese as the "good guys" made it impossible for us to, in the phrase current in the corridors of the State Department, "sell China down the river."

On January 27, 1941, the U.S. Embassy sent a telegram, later to become famous, reporting a rumor from the Peruvian ambassador that the Japanese military had planned a mass attack on Pearl Harbor to be executed in case of "trouble" with the United States. We in the embassy expected that the Japanese might make a grab in Southeast Asia. Grew worried that the United States would not fight to save Singapore, which he regarded as vital to our interests. But in our minds a direct assault on American territory would be insane and therefore unthinkable. We now know that studies for the Pearl Harbor raid were under way in Japan at the time we sent our telegram and that the Japanese Naval General Staff had at first rejected the proposal. When in October I returned to the United States via Hawaii, I was informed that the U.S. Navy had stepped up its reconnaissance of the islands on the basis of our message.

Ambassador Grew had faith in the efficacy of diplomacy. He believed that, in the end, the Japanese were reasonable people and that "constructive conciliation" was possible. In May the State Department asked him whether the Japanese would observe an agreement, if one were reached with the United States. Grew recorded in his diary that his reply was "perhaps the most important telegram" he had sent from Tokyo, drafted "early in the morning after a night of most careful and prayerful thought." His answer was affirmative: that a bilateral undertaking, sanctioned by the army and navy and approved by the cabinet, the privy council, and the emperor, would be carried out in good faith. Hornbeck in Washington disagreed. He believed that certain Japanese were trying to pull the wool over Grew's eyes, that the country's leaders were bent on expansion, and good faith could not be presumed.

The crisis of the summer of 1941 was the freezing of Japanese assets in the United States. I wrote to my wife, "On July 26 things happened. It was Saturday. The announcement of Japanese entry into French Indochina was made at noon and by two o'clock we heard that the United States government had frozen Japanese assets in the United States. There was much flurry in the *taishikan* (embassy) as you can imagine. That night the ambassador remarked that it was quite unusual to find the whole staff of secretaries in the office at 7:30 on a Saturday night!" The freezing order underscored the difficulties facing Japan and confirmed, in Japanese eyes, the fact of ABCD (American-British-Chinese-Dutch) encirclement.

Meanwhile, top secret conversations continued between Secretary of State Cordell Hull and Ambassador Nomura Kichisaburo in Washington and between Ambassador Grew and Prime Minister Konoye Fumimaro in Tokyo. No one in the embassy except the ambassador and counselor was supposed to know of the talks, but I managed to read the telegrams. Grew was encouraged when Konoye proposed in August that he meet President Roosevelt "somewhere in the Pacific." The drama of such an encounter appealed to FDR, who probably imagined a "Pacific Charter" to complement the Atlantic Charter which he had signed with Winston Churchill. The Lord Privy Seal, Marquis Kido Koichi, had cautioned Konoye about the gravity of Japan's situation, emphasizing the disparity between strength and goals and advising an adjustment of relations with the United States.

Hornbeck and his associates in the State Department's Office of Far Eastern Affairs took a jaundiced view of the suggested Konoye-Roosevelt rendezvous, to be held on an American warship off Alaska. They insisted that a general agreement should be reached *before* the conference, in order to insure its success. For the Japanese, this was impossible. Konoye could not, in advance, convince the military chiefs to support an accord that would inevitably have included some withdrawals of military forces from China and other minimum concessions. Konoye's only hope would have been to secure an on-the-spot agreement which, with the concurrence of the military officers accompanying him, and with the emperor's sanction, could have been presented as a *fait accompli* in Tokyo, in the form of an imperial rescript. This would have been possible, of course, only if the United States government had been willing to ask for less than the complete withdrawal of Japanese troops from China.

From April 1941 Hull had insisted on his four principles: 1) respect for the territorial integrity and sovereignty of all nations; 2) non-interference in the internal affairs of other countries; 3) equality, including equality of commercial opportunity; and 4) non-disturbance of the status quo in the Pacific except as the status quo might be altered by peaceful means. Grew reported, after a secret meeting with Konoye on September 6, that the prime minister, and thus the Japanese government, had "conclusively and wholeheartedly" accepted Hull's principles. Konoye recorded that the principles were "splendid" (*kekko*), that he agreed with them "in principle," but that a meeting with President Roosevelt would be necessary to work out certain problems.

Hull's principles were confronted by Japan's realities: raw materials, China, military power. The Japanese were not used to moralizing or to accepting general concepts as guides for action. Their wartime slogans were not principles but symbols to clothe actions the government was already taking. It is perhaps unproductive to speculate on what would have happened had a battleship meeting between Konoye and Roosevelt taken place. Probably no agreement would have been reached, given the rigidity of Japan's military, the unbending attitude of the American government toward the observance of principles, and the preoccupation of United States policymakers with China. Japan's military leaders might well have placed obstacles to any concessions that Konoye might have been prepared to make, although they were keenly conscious of the country's predicament and the need for a quick solution, by peaceful means, if not by war.

The situation was tense in Tokyo in the fall months of 1941. Dependents of U.S. government officials had been evacuated by the beginning of the year; the wives and children of private Americans and others without urgent business in Asia had been strongly advised by the United States government to leave the Far East. Our embassy community was one of enforced bachelors and single employees. Police surveillance of foreigners, especially Americans, was intensified. One's Japanese friends feared to come to the embassy and it was not politic to seek them out. We sensed the danger of hostilities and were convinced that, if pushed, the Japanese would fight. War would probably erupt in Southeast Asia.

Hornbeck believed that by turning the screws we could force the Japanese into submission, that a tough attitude would cause them to abandon their aims in Asia. When I returned to Washington in late October and, as was the custom, paid a courtesy call on Mr. Hornbeck, the senior official in the State Department concerned with Asia, he asked me, rhetorically, since he had read the stream of telegrams and despatches we had sent from Tokyo, "What do you people in the embassy think about war with Japan?" I replied without hesitation: "We think Japan wants to dominate East Asia and hopes to do so without war. But if this looks impossible, Japan will go to war in desperation." Hornbeck looked at me with derision, "Name me one country which has ever gone to war in desperation." No apt example came to mind and the conversation ended quickly. As the record shows, a few days after my interview with him, Hornbeck, on November 27, committed himself to a prediction: "In the opinion of the undersigned, the Japanese government does not desire or intend or expect to have armed conflict with the United States."

We did not anticipate an attack on Pearl Harbor. Unfortunately, we had forgotten the Peruvian ambassador's rumor. We in the State Department thought on that weekend of December 6–7 that an armed action might well take place in Southeast Asia, probably in Indochina, or to secure a foothold in the Netherlands East Indies. We were not, as I recall, as complacent as Hornbeck. In his defense, he later explained that his judgment of November 27 had been based on his "scrutiny of materials which emanated from 'intelligence' sources, some British and some American." These, of course, must have included the Japanese official cable traffic, decoded under the system known as MAGIC.

Both sides made mistaken judgments of each other. The Americans underestimated Japanese strength and determination; the Japanese convinced themselves that the United States, after receiving a knockout blow at Pearl Harbor, would not pursue them to the far reaches of the western and southern Pacific.

The basic conflict was still one between principles and realities. We insisted upon Japan's commitment to support our principles, and Pearl Harbor forced us to go to war over their failure to do so. By territorial and administrative integrity, we meant the integrity of

China. Reduced to its simplest terms, war with Japan would be a war about China, and also a war with Southeast Asia. We did not realize the extent of the "desperation" that would motivate the Japanese if they saw their national objectives—their security and their economic welfare—jeopardized. The Pearl Harbor attack manifested this desperation—an explosion which became a kind of Japanese national *seppuku* (the traditional method by which a Japanese warrior committed suicide through disembowelment).

Japan was to endure four years of hardship and misery before capitulating to Allied troops in August of 1945. For the first time in her long history, she had to submit to the occupation of her land by foreign military forces.

Occupation and Independence

The occupation began in August 1945 when the vanguard of the American army landed at an airfield near Tokyo. They were driven in Japanese transport to Yokohama, which was to be the headquarters of the Eighth Army. As they entered what was left of the city they observed few spectators among the ruins. At every intersection stood a Japanese soldier, rifle and bayonet at the ready, with his back to the convoy. This was a precaution against any possible attack or demonstration. On the whole, it was a dismal scene, suggestive of little triumph for the victors. The desolation was heightened, if anything, by the fact that the electric trains were still running along the embankment on the main line to Tokyo.

After the emperor's broadcast, which called upon the nation to "endure the unendurable," all kinds of rumors about the Americans had begun to spread among the people. There was a general belief that the occupying troops, filled with hatred of the Japanese, would be unrestrained in their behavior toward life and property. Many people, especially women, thought it prudent to leave Tokyo and Yokohama before the Americans moved in. But as the troops arrived by sea and air, it was soon evident that popular fears were groundless. The Americans did not act like demons at all. So began perhaps the most peaceful and, to outward appearances, the most harmonious occupation of one country by another that has ever been known.

Japan had never known defeat, much less occupation. Its people, not surprisingly, had no idea as to how they should conduct themselves in a situation that lacked all precedent. Moreover, they were confused, dazed, weary, and hungry. Most of them were too relieved that the war was over to cherish much resentment against those who had defeated them, especially when the enemy turned out to be far less vindictive than they had feared. Popular resentment, insofar as it existed at all, was directed against their national leaders, in particular the generals and admirals who had led Japan into a hopeless war.

Japan's devastating defeat turned the nation pacifist. The horrors of destruction and more than eight million casualties left the Japanese stunned and ready to welcome surcease from their agonies. The occupation was a relief and the Japanese cooperated fully. General MacArthur as Supreme Commander, in his pompous, arrogant, and aloof way, filled the vacuum left by the destruction of leadership and of the emperor's loss of perpetual sanctity inherited from his ancestors.

The people began to pick up their lives from the rubble, and the cleanup and rebuilding went according to careful planning with cooperation from the American troops. During the first five years, the United States contributed $1.7 billion to relief. The energies of the vast American occupation apparatus were concentrated on the disarmament, demilitarization, and democratization of Japan. Arms were destroyed, individual freedoms were restored, militarism was stamped out, and economic recovery was set in motion.

The U.S. Refashions Japan

Reforms, long planned by the government in Washington, were swiftly instituted. On October 4, 1945, a month after the surrender, the so-called "Bill of Rights" directive was issued by the Supreme Commander of the Allied Powers (SCAP), guaranteeing, among other rights, freedom of speech, assembly, religion, and political activity, and providing for the release of political prisoners. The election law was amended to lower the voting age from twenty-five to twenty and to guarantee the right of suffrage to women. Land reform was ordered, the educational system restructured, and State Shinto was abolished; in fact, every phase of Japanese society was changed on the basis of directives written in Washington and carried out by zealous SCAP personnel, imbued with the missionary zeal of creating a new nation. War criminals were tried and a purge of 200,000 bureaucrats undertaken to cleanse the government of "ultra-nationalists" and "undesirable persons." The revision of the constitution was perhaps the most important act of the occupation. Drafted in Mac-Arthur's Government Section, it provided for a parliamentary system, made the Diet the preeminent organ of government, leveled the emperor to a "symbol," and included the soon-to-be-famous Article 9, which abolished war potential and prohibited armies, navies, and air forces. Nearly forty years after its promulgation, no single comma of the text of the constitution has been altered by the Japanese.

Political parties mushroomed in their newfound freedom but, in spite of the Communists becoming legal for the first time in history, it was soon obvious that they were not the wave of the future, although many conservative Japanese blamed occupation authorities for liberating them and making communism possible in Japan. MacArthur was anxious to hold elections as soon as possible; the first one took place in April 1946, scarcely seven months after the end of the war. A second election was held a year later on April 25, 1947. In the first election, the conservatives won; in the second, the progressives gained most seats and the result was a weak coalition government, which, under two successive prime ministers, lasted less than a year and a half. Yoshida Shigeru, who became known as "One Man Yoshida" because of his pugnacious style, held office as prime minister for a year (May 1946–May 1947) and then served four successive terms from October 1948 to December 1954. In 1955 the Liberal Party and the Democratic Party merged to form the Liberal Democratic Party, which has maintained power continuously ever since.

In the election of 1949, the Communists attained thirty-five seats in the House of Representatives and won 10 percent of the vote; they were not to reach such strength again until 1972 when they captured forty seats, after which they steadily declined. In recent years, the Japan Communist Party (JCP) has usually captured no more than 4 to 5 percent of the vote. The temporary surge in 1972 was due to a combination of factors: the promise of the return of Okinawa—a prominent plank in the JCP platform—and the party's break with the Chinese and the Soviet Communist parties, which gave them a hoped-for image of independence in the public eye. Their attempt to present the face of a "lovable Communist party" and thereby win votes failed.

From 1945 to 1952, the year in which the occupation ended, the popular attitude toward SCAP was a compound of apprehension, admiration, disappointment, and boredom. These several emotions represent, in the order in which they have just been listed, the stages through which the Japanese, speaking in the broadest sense, passed in their reaction to the occupation as a whole. The later stages of disappointment and boredom were partly due to the length of the occupation.

As homes were rebuilt and as economic conditions improved, it was inevitable that the early enthusiasm for American ways should be succeeded by some reaction. Although at first very much worse had been expected, it was only natural that after five years people should get tired of seeing foreign uniforms in the streets and that retention by the Americans of commandeered houses, hotels, and railway stock should become irritating. There was yet another cause for the change in the popular attitude as the years went by: The policy of SCAP toward Japan underwent an important alteration three years after the occupation began. It was apparent that in the future the main aim of the occupation would be to rebuild Japan as an ally of the United States in the struggle against communism. Rehabilitation and revival became much more important than reform.

As the 1940s wore on and U.S. relations with the Soviet Union began to deteriorate, Japanese-American relations veered increasingly toward rebuilding Japan rather than emphasizing the reformation of the country. SCAP paid less attention to the implementation of the laws breaking up the *zaibatsu* or industrial combines. The outbreak of the Korean War in June 1950 was a watershed; MacArthur at once ordered the formation of a "police force" to guard a Japan denuded of American troops who were sent off to Korea. In September 1950 John Foster Dulles began preparing a peace treaty, and on April 10, 1951, President Truman dismissed MacArthur for insubordination. General MacArthur, as the Korean War progressed, had become increasingly critical of Washington's strategy and wrote letters to sympathetic congressmen and senators venting his anger over the way the war was being directed from the State Department and the Pentagon. His accusations became so flagrant that President Truman finally decided he had to go.

The dismissal of the Supreme Commander of the Allied Powers was an event that stunned the Japanese. It was to shape public attitudes toward the Japanese military in the postwar years and was to register in the Japanese psyche the belief that civilian control of Japan's new Self Defense Forces would prevent a reoccurrence of the militarism of the 1930s. If the Japanese needed a lesson in "civilian control," the firing of MacArthur, whom they had revered as the "Supreme Authority," was one to be burned into their consciousness. They were shocked, awed, and, in the end, filled with admiration. The principle of "civilian control," which had no Japanese equivalent, has been written into the charter of their Self-Defense Forces and is one of which they are constantly reminded. Of all events of the occupation, this one may have had the most profound effect on the Japanese.

Japan Regains Independence

On September 8, 1951, the treaty of peace was signed in San Francisco, and on the same day Japanese and American delegates convened at the Presidio to endorse the mutual security treaty that would guarantee Japan's security and provide for the stationing of American military forces in Japan.

As the years passed, dissatisfaction with the security treaty and disapproval of the presence of American bases and GI's on Japanese soil produced adverse reactions, spurred by the radical student movement. The protest movement culminated in the riots of 1960, in which a girl student was killed, the Diet was besieged, and Prime Minister Kishi resigned after having forcibly accomplished ratification of the newly revised treaty by the Diet. President Eisenhower's planned state visit to Japan was cancelled as a result.

A curious ambivalence of attitude was demonstrated by these rioting students. While much criticism and antagonism were directed at "the Americans," whenever the relationship was reduced to one-on-one, there was little evidence that the protesters were angry. Several of my student friends who were most vehement in their protests against U.S. policy toward Japan took pains to assure me that their actions in no way changed their feelings of friendship for me.

Although the 1960s started out inauspiciously, the decade saw the beginning of the remarkable economic growth that was to bring Japan in a few years to the position of third greatest economic power in the world. In 1962, the Gross National Product (GNP) was already three times that of the prewar period 1934–1936. Ikeda Hayato, who became prime minister after Kishi's downfall, announced his policy of the "low posture" (*teishisei*), meaning that Japan would concentrate on its economic development and avoid international quarrels. The pageant that fittingly symbolized Japan's "coming of age" in the postwar world was the staging in Tokyo of the Olympic Games of 1964. The Japanese outdid themselves in refurbishing and improving Tokyo as no other people could do; they were to be on display for the whole world to see, and in those few days of color and athletic prowess Japan dramatically demonstrated that it was a nation which the world would learn to respect in the future.

Okinawa became a more pressing problem. Although the Pentagon and the State Department did not always see eye to eye on the necessity to return the islands to Japan as soon as possible, the movement toward reversion could not be slowed or stopped. Finally, on May 15, 1972, Okinawa became a prefecture of the Japanese homeland, although rights for the continued stationing of American military forces were granted by Japan. The Japanese emphatically demanded that no nuclear weapons be stored on the islands and this became, for them, a fixed condition of the agreement.

Japan's defeat did not put to rest her problems with China. The U.S. Senate in 1952, for example, refused to ratify the U.S.-Japan peace treaty if Communist China were invited to participate. Prime Minister Yoshida wanted to avoid a choice between the two Chinas—one on the mainland, the other on Taiwan. But the ultimatum was clear and Japan signed a treaty with the government of Chiang Kai-shek on Taiwan. When the United States decided to change its policy in 1971, Japan, which had faithfully observed the U.S. principle of non-recognition of mainland China, was not consulted. Secretary of State Rogers telephoned Ambassador Ushiba Nobuhiko in Washington on July 15, 1971, to inform him that within about thirty minutes, President Nixon would go on the air in Washington to announce his forthcoming visit to meet Mao Tse-tung in Peking. This, which became known as the "China Shock," deeply irritated the Japanese, who felt that their proximity and close historical relationship with China, let alone their past unswerving following of America's lead in Asian policy, entitled them to more consideration. The shock was compounded when we later failed to consult or notify Japan of succeeding basic changes in our economic policy.

The Shanghai communique was issued on February 27, 1972, during President Nixon's visit to China. The two key sentences read: "The United States acknowledges that all Chinese on either side of the Taiwan strait maintain there is but one China and that Taiwan is a part of China. The United States government does not challenge that position." A few months later, in September, Prime Minister Tanaka visited Peking and, going farther than President Nixon, extended full diplomatic recognition to the People's Republic of China. The United States could not do this so easily because of our treaty with the Republic of China on Taiwan. Seven years later, in 1979, the United States denounced this treaty and extended full recognition to the PRC. Meanwhile Japan, in October 1978, signed a "treaty of peace and friendship" with the government of mainland China.

Those of us who worked in the American Embassy in Tokyo in the 1960s (both authors were there), were preoccupied principally with two problems: security and trade. Today, in the 1980s, the U.S. is still concerned mainly with these two problems. They are both the foundations and the irritants in a relationship that has long been called a "partnership" and has only recently been accepted by both governments as an "alliance." It is to these two elements of the alliance that we now turn.

CHAPTER 5

The phenomenal invasion of American markets by Japan has fueled the trade dispute. Over half of the automobiles driven by Californians, for example, are Japanese made; Japanese watches are worn on the wrists of a majority of Los Angeles and San Francisco residents; 90 percent of U.S. homes have TV sets made by Japanese companies; IBM is struggling to maintain its lead over the Japanese in the computer field; and most of the radios, electric shavers, and video cassette recorders are stamped "made in Japan." Sometime over the next year, Los Angeles County is likely to become the first American municipal government to borrow Japanese yen. It would thus join a host of big corporate borrowers, among them IBM and Walt Disney, that are taking advantage of low Japanese interest rates. And the invasion appears to be accelerating.

(The above is a collage of statements excerpted from U.S. newspapers and periodicals.)

TRADE: JAPAN CHALLENGES THE UNITED STATES

Those of us who returned to Japan in the early days of the occupation can never forget the bleak pessimism with which we all viewed the future of Japan. One had only to look across the huge areas of space and rubble in Tokyo and the other principal cities, with the exception of Kyoto, to be convinced that a modern, industrialized country could never rise again. We pessimists were wrong. We could not have foreseen how determination, hard work, and dedication would produce a Japanese economic miracle. To look for answers to Japan's amazing economic success and the challenge she now poses to the United States, we need to go back again to the 1860s, when the foundations were laid for Japan's industrialization.

The Economic Rise

We noted in Chapter 3 how with the Meiji Restoration, Japan turned an important historical corner in 1868 and began the long struggle to throw off the shackles of feudalism and build a modern state. Even before this momentous event, there were stirrings of modernization. The rise of an active merchant class during the time that Japan was closed to the outside world and the presence of numerous able, eager, unemployed young samurai helped to meet the challenge of the opening of the rest of the world to commercial intercourse. Many enterprising Japanese had studied Dutch and through Dutch merchants had learned something about the industry and commerce of Europe and America. Some of the feudal lords had established factories and schools.

The determination of the Meiji founders to build a rich country and a strong military was translated into a feverish absorption in learning and applying the secrets of an industrial West. Foreign trade started from zero in 1860 and reached 10 percent of the Gross National Product by 1900. (By 1983, Japan carried on 10 percent of the trade of the entire world!) Imports and exports doubled in the first decade after Emperor Meiji's assumption of rule in 1868. Trade continued to double in each of the first decades of the twentieth century. Exports and imports increased eightfold in volume in the period 1880 to 1913. The impulse for foreign trade was touched off by the need for raw materials and machinery.

The mood of the time has been described as "a craze for Occidental civilization . . . almost a pathological phenomenon." An astute foreign observer in Meiji times wrote on January 11, 1872: "Japan's record of progress for 1871 is noble. The Mikado's government is no longer an uncertainty. . . . Feudalism is dead . . . the swords of the samurai are laid aside. The peace and order throughout the country appear wonderful. Progress is everywhere the watchword. Is not this the finger of God?"

Economic expansion continued unabated until military involvement on the continent of China began to change the purpose and direction of the nation's economy. The resources of the colonies of Taiwan and Korea were mobilized, and after 1937, when the so-called "China Incident" erupted, the nation was to all intents and purposes on a war footing. In 1944, in the midst of the Great Pacific War (as it is called in Japan), defense expenditures amounted to 68 percent of the national income. The folly of Japan's embarcation on a war it could not win was cogently demonstrated in a communication addressed by Winston Churchill to Japanese Foreign Minister Matsuoka Yosuke, hand-delivered in Moscow by the British Ambassador to the Soviet Union, Sir Stafford Cripps, at a performance of the Moscow Art Theater in April 1941. The note specified facts for Japan to consider in weighing a decision for war or peace. One fact was a reminder that in contrast to Japan's annual production of 7 million tons of steel, the

United States and Great Britain together would produce 90 million tons of steel in 1941.

Postwar Recovery

Once the Japanese population had restored a semblance of normalcy to their lives and had begun to shake off the daze and despair which had gripped them, the traditional hard work ethic began to reassert itself. A per capita income of $46 in 1946 had multiplied almost eight times by 1950. The Korean War (1950–1953) provided a sharp spurt to Japan's economy, as American procurement for the war could be most efficiently and economically accomplished in Japan. The period thereafter, especially the 1960s, became Japan's takeoff for economic growth, averaging in excess of 10 percent per year throughout the decade. The 1970s brought the oil crises that Japan has been given credit for overcoming successfully through strict conservation measures, although energy is still a crucial problem.

Until 1965 the United States exported more goods to Japan than it imported from her, but in that year the balance turned the other way, causing the United States to suffer the mounting trade deficits that in recent years have been a major source of friction between the two countries. Before the war the Japanese were known for creating shoddy products and poor imitations of foreign manufactured goods. In the fresh air of surcease from battle, the erstwhile captains of industry seemed sworn to destroy forever their repugnant reputation for mediocrity. Trying by every means possible, especially through licensing arrangements for foreign technology—to a large degree from the United States—the Japanese succeeded in closing the ten-year gap in advances of production and technology that they had created by fighting a useless war. They worked passionately, as if to wreak revenge on those gods who had sent them into futile combat. Quality control, taught them by Americans, became the watchword. Industries in which the Japanese had never before been known as serious competitors began to export their manufactures into the United States in increasing quantities: iron and steel, metal products, machines, radios and television sets, automobiles, motorcycles, tape recorders, and cameras, as well as the traditional goods well-known in prewar days: toys, textiles, clothing, footwear, and frozen fish. Two-way trade in 1972 amounted to $14 billion, with a surplus for Japan of $4.9 billion.

It is little wonder that following a 1981 deficit of $16 billion, Representative Stephen J. Solarz, chairman of the House of Representatives Subcommittee on Asian and Pacific Affairs, convened hearings on United States-Japan relations, opening them on March 1, 1982, with the comment: "The Japanese-American relationship, our most important bilateral relationship in the world, is rapidly becoming one of the most controversial." By 1982 total trade had climbed to $60 billion, and the American deficit had mounted to $17 billion.

Let us look at some of the reasons for the enormous imbalance in U.S.-Japan trade. First, however, I want to explain the curious phenomenon of Japan's having a large trade surplus with the rest of the world, yet still suffering an accumulated national debt of over $500 billion that takes nearly 40 percent of the Gross National Product to service. Japan's current trade surplus with the United States, which is edging up to nearly $70 billion in 1987, represents profits held by Japanese companies—Toyota, Sony, Matsushita, Nissan, to name a few—not revenue for the Japanese government. The government must obtain its income, just as the United States government does, through taxation. While corporate taxes are high in Japan, so are national expenditures. The Japanese government subsidizes expensive social welfare and national medical programs, supports education and local government with sizeable grants, carries out extensive public works programs, and increasingly allocates more funds for defense. Taxes do not cover all these expenses, so the government sells bonds to banks, insurance companies, and individual citizens. Annual interest paid on these bonds is what is known as debt service and it is this service that contributes in substantial measure to the large national debt.

Staples of U.S.-Japan Trade

One of the first causes of the imbalance, and therefore the controversy, is the difference in the nature of the goods we trade with each other. We ship necessary raw materials that are unavailable in Japan; Japan sells us its highly advanced manufactured goods of superb quality that compete directly with American products. In 1982, out of a total U.S. export figure to Japan of $20.6 billion, $12.4 billion (or nearly two-thirds) represented raw materials. Of Japan's total exports to the United States of $37.7 billion, more than 95 percent (or $36 billion) consisted of manufactured goods, including machinery, automobiles, telecommunications equipment, office machinery and equipment, and miscellaneous manufactures. In office machinery and computers alone, Japan's sales to us were $2 billion; our exports to Japan of comparable machines were valued at $1.2 billion. As Representative Solarz noted, "With the single exception of airplanes, no manufactured civilian product imported from the United States has as much as 10 percent of the Japanese market."

Agriculture

A not infrequent sarcastic observation is that with respect to Japan, the United States is in the position of a developing country, selling its agricultural produce and raw materials and receiving highly sophisticated equipment in return. Agricultural commodities are highest on our list of exports to Japan, amounting each year to between $6 and $7 billion. American farmers are content that Japan is their best customer. American foodstuffs account for a quarter of Japan's caloric intake; it has been estimated that one out of every twenty acres cultivated in the United States produces food for Japan. In 1973, when because of a bad soybean crop the United States temporarily cut off shipments of soybeans to Japan, a crisis in Japanese-American relations erupted—to the surprise of most Americans, who are unaware that soybeans are a staple of life for the Japanese and that 95 percent of their soybean needs are imported from the United States.

It is ironic that a trade in which the Japanese are the world's greatest consumers of American products should produce frictions over exports from the United States of such items as beef and oranges. As the first Japan-United States Economic Relations Group, dubbed the "Wise Men," stated in its 1981 report, "In the United States, Japanese quotas on citrus fruits and beef have become symbolic of Japanese agricultural protectionism." Although between 1965 and 1979 import quotas on agricultural and marine products were reduced, the spotlight has been kept on maintaining the quotas on citrus and beef. Japan's 350,000 beef-cattle-producing farm households have demanded protection for their industries, and the growers of mandarin oranges (*mikan*) have insisted that free introduction of oranges would put them out of business. Yet ironically, forty-four of the fifty U.S. states prohibit the import of *mikans*.

In actuality, it is the Japanese consumer who suffers. Prices of beef are beyond the reach of the less affluent households, and, just as the liberalization of lemons produced no ripples in Japan's economy, free imports of oranges would enrich the Japanese diet and probably have little effect on the popularity of the traditional *mikan*. As it is, Japan in

1980 imported 57.6 percent of total U.S. beef exports, providing the largest market for U.S. beef, and purchased 14.7 percent of total U.S. orange exports. Yet with the ever-looming trade crisis, the United States continues to urge Japan to purchase more beef and citrus fruits. As beef distribution is tightly controlled by the Japanese meat syndicate, prices are very high compared to the United States. This is the cause of much consumer grumbling in Japan but there is little evidence that the beef industry has loosened its grip on the marketing of beef in Japan. A White House source was quoted as saying that Japan is no longer just a cornerstone of our Asian policy: "It is our primary partner on the global stage. We simply cannot allow the 'beef and citrus syndrome' to trivialize and embitter the relationship."

The Japanese agricultural lobby is small but powerful, and the voices of protectionism in the U.S. Congress and labor unions are rising higher. In Japan, the labor unions, interested in the production and export of machinery and industrial equipment, have little or no sympathy for the farmers. The president of the Japanese National Iron and Steel Workers Federation in a recent newspaper article denounced the farmers for their "egoistic opposition to liberalization," and concluded that the time had come for the government to carry out liberalization. The problem of beef and oranges has yet to be solved.

Productivity

The Japanese and American "Wise Men," in their 1981 report to the president and prime minister, concluded that the president should make productivity a major issue of United States economic policy. Productivity is a measure of the economy of a nation, usually defined by the output per man-hour or the GNP (Gross National Product) per worker. The gap in the growth rate of productivity between Japan and the United States has been one of the most discussed elements in the trade friction that has developed between the two countries in the last few years. The statistics provide the reason: The rate of growth in labor productivity in the manufacturing field between 1973 and 1979 was 45 percent in Japan and 7 percent in the United States. These rates have not changed appreciably.

Various factors explain Japan's high productivity growth in contrast to that of the United States. One is the ferocious spirit and technique of competition that has developed in domestic as well as in foreign markets. Rivalry among Japanese companies producing similar products can reach great heights, although the government, especially through the Ministry of International Trade and Industry (MITI), can by "administrative guidance" sometimes bring order into the marketplace and blunt the sharpest controversies. In spite of Japan's reputation for "flooding the markets of the world," in 1979 it exported only 12.6 percent of its GNP, which is smaller than most industrial countries except the United States, whose exports in the same year amounted to only 12.2 percent of its GNP.

Research & Development and Technology

Rivalry with Japan has been intense in the whole area of research and development (R&D) and technology. The transfer of technology between the two nations has been a particular focus of controversy. Since the end of the war, the transfer of technology, particularly defense-related technology, has been a one-way street—from the United States to Japan. The United States has had an advantage in R & D in the past because much of its defense technology has produced a spin-off for commercial use. This advantage has declined, however, as military and commercial technology have become more sharply differentiated. Within the past two years the advanced state of Japanese technology has lured the U.S. Defense Department to regard with envy some of the advanced "high-tech" products in which the Japanese have become the forerunners.

Japan, observing faithfully Article 9 of its constitution prohibiting military forces and war potential, established in 1976 a policy of banning any sales of weapons or defense technology to any nation without exception. Americans regard the Mutual Security Treaty between Japan and the United States and the long history of American-generated military aid and sales programs as justification for a relaxation of the ban in the case of the United States. But the issue in Japan is political, and the opposition parties and some members of the ruling Liberal Democratic party have been reluctant to make an exception to the prohibition, even for their ally—the United States. The opposition is always fearful that any change in the interpretation of laws regarding security matters could be the opening wedge in the government's efforts to build up Japan's military forces.

Finally, in January 1983, Prime Minister Nakasone, having long favored a reasonable defense force for Japan, agreed to the sale of Japanese weapons technologies to the United States. Meetings between defense experts of the two countries have since been held to work out the details of the arrangement. One special technology that has interested the U.S. Defense Department is the science of fiber-optics, of which Japan's computer industry has been the leading developer. New advances provide high-speed communications links by which a large variety of information is transmitted, including voices, images, and data transformed into optic signals. In August 1983 the Japanese Construction Ministry announced plans to lay optical fiber cables along highways in order to establish a communications network to help solve such problems as traffic congestion, pollution (involving noise and auto gases), and to provide information services for highway drivers. Optic fibers are useful for military purposes because they form ultra-high-speed communication links, utilizing light waves that cannot be jammed or overheard by enemy agents.

Another technology interesting to the United States is ferrite paint, of which the Japanese company TDK is the top manufacturer. These ferrite materials could be used to coat the radar-proof "stealth bomber" being developed by the United States. Other items desired by the Pentagon are very large-scale integrated circuits, charge-coupled devices for detecting infrared rays, and the latest random-access memory chip manufactured by Hitachi and Mitsubishi.

The U.S. government has a slight edge over private industry in R & D outlays, including military expenditures: 50.4 percent against 49.6 percent. Japan's R & D effort is, as might be expected, overwhelmingly conducted in the private sector: 72 percent against 28 percent of government expenditures. Since the war Japan has, of course, benefited from American technology, and some companies in recent years have let their zeal extend to illegal practices in obtaining American know-how. With a few exceptions, such as Nobel Prize winner Yukawa Hideo, a physicist, Japan's R & D performance has been more in the form of production technology and group efforts than in fundamental, trail-blazing innovation by individuals. Recently the United States and Japan have engaged in a number of cooperative efforts in research and development; as many as forty-eight projects are now being carried out in such diverse fields as energy, space, health and medicine, environment, agriculture, and pure scientific research. Unfortunately, U.S. expenditures on R & D declined from 3 percent of GNP in the 1960s to 2.2 percent in the 1970s, largely due to a reduction in government-funded research. The "Wise Men" have pointed out that declines in R & D have long-term implications for growth of productivity, slowing the entire innovation process.

Patent applications are a measure of research and development in the technological field. During the first twenty years after the end of the war, Japan necessarily depended on imported technology, especially through licensing arrangements, to build the foundation blocks for industry. After 1965, the year the trade balance shifted in favor of Japan, it became clear that to achieve success in a world of rapidly advancing technology, Japan would have to work toward greater independence from foreign inventions. During the period 1966–1980, applications for patent rights in Japan doubled—from 86,000 to 191,000. During the same time, American applications increased slightly—from 89,000 to 104,000—while those in West Germany declined. In this fourteen-year period, applications from Japan for foreign patent rights tripled, from 10,000 to 35,000, while those from the United States and Western Europe declined.

American private sector R & D expenditures have been criticized for focusing too much on regulatory compliance and product differentiation rather than on the development of new products and processes, in contrast to the accomplishments of the Japanese. There appears, however, to be a new surge in Yankee inventiveness and a new determination, inspired no doubt by the phenomenal success of the Japanese and the overpowering publicity given to Japanese quality control, "Zen-type" management procedures, and aggressive penetration of the marketplace.

The United States still holds the lead in the semi-conductor industry and experts expect it to remain ahead for some time. The battle of the "chips" is still ahead, however, and one can be sure that the fight will be intense. Professor Daniel I. Okimoto of Stanford University has compared the semi-conductor industries in Japan and the United States, labeling the latter the "pioneer" and Japan the "pursuer." He concludes: "While Japan's accomplishments to date are truly noteworthy, given the distance that has been traversed and the obstacles overcome, the real test lies ahead: Can Japan's semi-conductor industry make the tough transition from pursuer to pioneer?"

Computers

In the past, Japan's greatest successes have come from taking others' ideas or products and improving or redesigning them to make them commercially feasible for a mass market. This has been true of the transistor, the video tape recorder, the small car, the motorcycle (the Japanese have captured 90 percent of the U.S. market), and even their much vaunted "quality control." Newer generations of Japanese are convinced that the future lies in new and original scientific break-throughs, which require a different kind of mentality and approach than the traditional Japanese way of absorbing someone else's cul-ture—as they did from the Chinese, from the Western world when opened to them, and from the American occupiers.

The English word "vision" has become popular in Japan, and new "visions" of the future are periodically produced and published. MITI published a "vision" a few years ago, outlining the steps that Japan should take to cope with a "new age." The Science and Technology Agency has, since 1970, produced three "visions," the latest of which prognosticates such breathtaking goals as a method for managing ra-dioactive waste by 1994, three-dimensional television by 1997, eradi-cation of cancer by 2001, hydrogen-powered cars by 2008, and solar-power plants in space by the same year. Such projections illustrate the new Japanese concentration on high technology as the wave of the future and as a way out of some of the problems that will inevitably befall Japan as the new millenium dawns: the inevitable decline of labor-intensive industries, the slipping of the work ethic into a "pleas-ure ethic" for the younger generation, and an aging population that is living longer but working less.

American scientists do not lack for "visions." It was announced on August 15, 1983, that the High Energy Physics Advisory Panel, a body attached to the U.S. Department of Energy, had proposed the con-struction of the world's largest accelerator, called a "super super-conducting collider," which would enable scientists to study the basic nature of the universe. Built on the scale of the present Capitol Belt-way (freeway) around Washington, DC, the machine would cost be-tween $1 and $2 billion and would require ten years to construct. The project would require both government and private cooperation, and the necessary research and development would cost between $150 and $200 million. The Department of Energy is apparently looking into the possibilities "with great interest."

Robotics

Possessing an estimated 70 percent of the world's robots, Japan is leading the "robot revolution," the future implications of which are not only economic but social and cultural as well. Never having ac-cepted a monotheistic religion (worshipping a "personal God"), the Japanese can accept robots on the factory floor more easily than can non-Japanese. The Shinto beliefs that gods are in everything—in stones, trees, and mountains—make it possible to work comfortably with machines that perform humanlike tasks but do not threaten. This idea may be tenable as philosophy, especially to the Japanese, but it contrasts with the concept of a usurper of man's rightful place, perhaps a more prevalent reaction among Western workers whose jobs may be at stake. Acceptance and the integration of robots into the workplace have thus far worked fairly smoothly in Japan, but the U.S. is still in the early stages of the robot revolution.

The technological transition, especially in robotics, is further eased in Japan by the compatible relationship between labor and management that prevails in most Japanese companies. Union and company have each other's interests at heart and avoid confrontation whenever possible. However, the first glimmerings of trouble in labor-management relations have emerged in an agreement signed in March 1983 between Nissan Motor Company and its labor union of 47,000 members, in which the company offered prior consultation in case of further automation and promised that the introduction of additional robots would not lead to the dismissal of workers, to demotions, or to less pay. Companies have thus far been able to handle these problems by transferring robot-displaced workers to more challenging jobs. The employee who has been performing the Charlie Chaplinlike mechanical motions on a production line will, of course, welcome a change to a more interesting function. But such appealing accommodations may not be possible as robotization goes on apace.

In fact, many workers in factories using robots who have been subjected to the transfer experience have become unhappy, and some have quit their jobs. Young laborers who supervise robots find mental strain in the loneliness of a job that prevents normal daily association with fellow employees in a conventional factory situation. One expert on labor relations has commented, "The psychological impact of automation is far greater than outside observers imagine." One is reminded of the speech in the 1921 play by Karel Capek, *R.U.R.*: "Robots of the world! The power of man has fallen! A new world has arisen: The Rule of the Robots! March!"

The economics of robotization are too powerful to ignore. As the president of a robot-leasing company in Japan explains: "It costs a firm 5 million yen ($21,000) a year for a skilled worker who is on the job only eight hours a day." For only twice that amount a manager can buy a robot that works round-the-clock. The arc-welding process used in shipbuilding and heavy manufacturing is an example of the effect of robots on productivity. Because of the time factor, robots welding an arc can effect a saving that will pay for a $100,000 welding robot in one year. Japan uses 1,000 arc-welding robots whereas there are only 100 in the United States.

Robots are being used increasingly in American factories, although robotization is far behind that of Japan. The United States operates approximately 5,000 robots against more than twice that many in Japan. General Motors is said to be the largest potential robot user in the United States, and plans to install 14,000 robots by 1990. At the same time, Matsushita Electric Industrial Company has announced that it expects to be using 100,000 robots by 1990. With the projected plans for expansion, Japanese robot manufacturers anticipate a $5 billion business by 1990. Americans are far from oblivious to the future challenges of robotics. There are said to be ninety-eight robot education programs now in existence in universities throughout the United States, and 190 universities have instituted research facilities for the exploration of the potential of robots.

Automobiles

The first "road wagon," or "horseless steam carriage," was invented by a Frenchman in about 1770 and was capable of maintaining a speed of two and one-half miles per hour, with frequent stops to make steam. It was a century later that a German invented the internal combustion engine, and the resulting "car" changed the history of the world. The United States soon took the lead in automobile production and the name of Henry Ford became a household word in the industrialized countries of the world. Annual American production of automobiles was over two million by 1938, and the ratio of population per vehicle was four to one in 1939. Of the leading countries of the world, Japan had the lowest proportionate number of automobiles: one vehicle per 389 persons.

In 1950 the United States produced 80 percent of the world's automobiles; in 1981 the percentage had declined to 30 percent. By 1982 the Japanese, who started their motor vehicle industry almost from scratch after the war, had captured 22.6 percent of total retail sales of automobiles in the United States. In 1986 the figure was closer to 25 percent. Toyota and Nissan have become the world's second and third top automakers in the world, still ceding first place to General Motors.

The automobile dispute with Japan has been one of the most sensitive and abrasive of all trade problems between the two countries.

The American has a proprietary feeling about the automobile, a "love affair with his car," as has often been stated. The controversy has been highly emotional, and understandably so, because of the connection easily and popularly drawn between Japanese imports and unemployment in the auto industry. Douglas A. Fraser, then president of the UAW (United Auto Workers of America), in testimony before the House subcommittees on International Policy and Trade and on Asian and Pacific Affairs in 1982, submitted a chart to show that during 1981–1982, thirty automotive plants in the United States had either been closed or their imminent closing announced, with a resulting 55,964 "jobs lost." Tensions have eased considerably recently with the yen having gained value, and prices for Japanese cars have risen accordingly. The establishment of Japanese automobile factories in the United States employing American workers has also helped to ease strains. Yet competition from Japan, South Korea, and West Germany keeps whittling away at Detroit's share of the American automobile market, causing continued lay-off of workers.

When the General Motors plant at Fremont, California, closed, television news coverage gave great prominence to stormy scenes of demonstrations, including a ballad sung by some of the workers, with the refrain, "We've lost our jobs to the Japanese!" Although it was subsequently announced that GM and Toyota had reached agreement for joint production at a reopened Fremont plant, long, drawnout bickering ensued among the companies and the UAW over union demands that its members be given job preference in rehiring for the new plant. Toyota particularly insisted that the plant should be regarded as a totally new venture and that no obligation existed to rehire former workers.

Final approval for the Toyota-GM joint venture was handed down by the Federal Trade Commission (FTC) on December 22, 1983, limiting production to 250,000 cars a year for a period of twelve years. As could be expected, reaction was divided. A laid-off worker at the Fremont plant cried, "Great news! Great news!" But Chairman Lee Iacocca of the Chrysler Corporation responded glumly, "The FTC is letting the two strongest automotive companies in the world monopolize the small car market. It's not right, and I will do everything in my power to see that the American public gets a clear picture of just how wrong it is." The FTC itself was not unanimous; one commissioner stated, "This joint venture is a plain and unambiguous violation of anti-trust laws."

An automobile analyst for a large brokerage firm attacked the GM-Toyota agreement as conceding the subcompact to Japan and neglecting, in return for immediate profit advantages to General Motors, America's strategic position in the manufacturing world. Another American writer, an automobile analyst and portfolio manager, draws an opposite conclusion—that the venture could have positive advantages for the United States by reversing the historic direction of technology transfer from the U.S. to Japan, and by motivating other American automobile companies to conclude similar agreements with Japanese affiliates. The writer calls the venture "the surest way for all to regain the competitiveness essential to the revitalization of our auto industry." Some time has passed since production began at the Fremont plant. From evidence available, the joint venture has been a success. Automobile production has increased, quality is up and in some cases has exceeded Japanese standards, and workers and management appear to be developing a satisfactory relationship.

One can understand the feelings of umemployed workers and their families and their natural inclination to blame the Japanese for selling competing cars whose popularity caused the closing of factories where they had worked for many years. The customer who buys a Japanese car because of the belief that it is more economical and better built than an American model is seldom blamed for his choice, which is the crucial factor. But there have been well-publicized scenes of destruction of Japanese cars by sledgehammers wielded by angry displaced workers and isolated threats to drivers of foreign cars.

The truth, of course, is that since the oil crisis of 1973 the small car has come into its own, and Americans who once reveled in their heavy, big-finned vehicles have turned to the inexpensive, easily maneuverable, small import. At the same time the Japanese cars have gained a reputation not only for fuel efficiency, but for excellent workmanship, attention to detail, and freedom from defects. In the face of numerous recalls of thousands of American models for one defect or another, one has not heard of the necessity to recall Japanese cars for repairs. In fact, according to the *Wall Street Journal*, Japanese rejections of machined parts are 1 percent of those in American counterpart plants.

As for productivity, a plant in Japan operated by Toyo Kogyo, third largest Japanese manufacturer of automobiles, claims to produce 20,000 complete cars and 7,000 partly assembled ones in one month, with two shifts of 900 workers each. By contrast, a Chrysler factory in Detroit employs 4,700 workers to make 20,000 cars per month.

There is, of course, another view about quality. Douglas Fraser never fails to argue that the Japanese car is less safe than an American car of like size and weight: "You are less apt to suffer serious injury or fatality." He adds that American vehicles are more rust-resistant than their Japanese counterparts because of the use of a "thicker gage [sic] metal" and the galvanizing of the steel, "which the Japanese are not yet doing."

The cost advantage the Japanese enjoy in selling automobiles to the United States is made up of a number of elements. The table* below prepared for the *New York Times* and published in February 1983 outlines the items in dollars per car. There has been little substantial change in these statistics.

A plan to limit Japanese competition in automobiles is the so-called local content law, or "Fair Practices in Automotive Products Act."

Cost Factors	Cost savings per car	Total Cost savings per car
Superior technology	$ 73	$ 73
Better management systems		
Quality control	329	
"Just-in-time" production techniques	550	
Materials, handling, engineering	41	
Other (quality circles, jobs classification)	476	1,396
Union-management relations		
Less absenteeism	81	
More flexible relief systems and allowances	89	
Union representation	12	182
Lower wages and fringe benefits		550
Total cost advantage to the Japanese		2,201
Less shipping costs		(484)
Net cost advantage to the Japanese		$1,717

*© 1983 by the New York Times Company. Reprinted by permission.

According to Douglas Fraser, "Companies with a high volume of car and truck sales in the U.S. would produce here, hire workers here, and buy auto parts made here." The percentage required by the content standards would increase in proportion to the sales of the Japanese companies in the United States. In short, the slogan is "Sell here, build here." Fraser estimated that the local "content" legislation requiring foreign automobile manufacturers to buy a certain percentage of parts from U.S. suppliers would create 868,000 auto and auto-related jobs in the United States by 1985.

American auto producers complain of the difficulty of selling U.S.-made cars in Japan. The total number of American cars sold in Japan in the twelve-month period ending March 31, 1983, was 3,145, half of sales in 1981. The American share in the Japanese market for cars is down to 9.2 percent, whereas six years ago, 1978, it was 37 percent. The Germans are in the lead with 76 percent of the import market. The American share of the market continues to dwindle.

The principal reasons American cars don't sell in Japan are not difficult to discern. American small cars cannot compete with the Japanese, who "invented" the small car. The standard American "gas guzzler," or big luxury automobile, is not suited for Japan's narrower roads and city streets. American manufacturers are poor at marketing and advertising and in establishing dealer outlets. The image of an American luxury car in Japan, once the acme of prestige, has lost its glamour and is no longer identified with the so-called "high-collar" class. On the contrary, its image has become associated with Japan's Mafia, the "Yakuza," who ostentatiously flaunt their wealth in the biggest American automobiles.

Another impediment an American car must overcome is the fact that thus far no American auto designer has bothered to concede that the Japanese drive on the left-hand side of the road and therefore the standard American left-hand drive is awkward for a Japanese.

When I was in Tokyo in the spring of 1987, I stood on a busy corner in the popular Ginza shopping district to count the number of American cars that passed. In thirty minutes, I saw two German cars, one Rolls Royce and no American automobiles. In talking with several Japanese friends later, it was explained that Japanese buy Japanese automobiles because they believe them to be better made, better serviced, and more comfortable to drive on narrower, congested Japanese roads. Despite evidence that Detroit is beginning to awaken to the realities of marketing automobiles abroad in the late 1980s (the

Ford Motor Company is doing extremely well in Europe), Japan continues to be a challenge to American car makers. Some analysts suggest that Detroit has given up on the Japanese market.

There are signs, however, that the American automobile industry has begun to profit from the competition with Japan. More attention is being given to quality control and workmanship. The effort to upgrade quality is on. As just one example, Buick has introduced computerized testing equipment in an aging plant in Flint, Michigan, an indication, according to the *New York Times*, of "the sweeping changes now underway in the once-complacent United States auto industry."

Even in the area of labor-management relations in the U.S. automobile industry, Japan's influence is being felt. The labor-management problem is a matter of the difference in the two systems. Japanese labor works *with* management; an adversarial relation is not the accepted pattern. Perhaps with the example of life-or-death competition before them American workers and bosses will decide that cooperation is better than confrontation. This is beginning to happen. Due to the continuation of the present upturn in American automobile profits, the example of the success of Japanese plants and joint ventures in the United States, and the expected economic recovery and advance in the United States and Japan, the future of the automobile industry in both countries may become brighter.

Industrial Policy

In the past few years a growing number of books have been published in the United States analyzing Japanese industrial policy and way of management and charting "lessons" the U.S. might learn from Japan's stellar performance. Much can be learned from Japan's methods, and seminars, university courses, and lectures have risen throughout the U.S., while visits to Japan of members of congress, academics, industrialists, and others hoping to penetrate the secrets of the traditionally considered "inscrutable" Japanese have proliferated. We are now "copying the copiers," those prewar makers of copied merchandise that was held in such disdain by foreigners. What we cannot copy is the tradition, the heritage, the nature of the Japanese which evolved over 2,000 years of history and which we have tried to adumbrate in the opening chapter of this book. Traditions from the past form part of us, although often unidentifiable.

In the words of a journalist writing in the *Asian Wall Street Journal*

Weekly, "'industrial policy' and 'targeting,' Washington's new buzz-words in the battle to liberalize Japanese trade policy, began to sound like a variation on the old U.S. concern with 'opening the Japanese market.'" "Industrial policy" has indeed become a concept central to the Japanese-American controversy over trade relations.

Until the end of the 1960s, the Japanese explained industrial policy as a necessity. It would enable them to meet international competition in the heavy and chemical industries and to promote exports in order to earn foreign exchange with which to import raw materials and primary products. Since the 1970s, influenced by changes in the international economy, including the repercussions of OPEC's 1972 oil shocks, Japanese industrial policy has focused on the decline of the "smokestack" or "sunset" industries and also encouraged the emergence and development of the "sunshine" industries (i.e., iron and steel, textiles) based on high technology. The Japanese look on these efforts as made not so much under dictation from the government or the Ministry of International Trade and Industry (MITI), but as emerging from the acceptance and positive cooperation of the private sector, both labor and management. To the Japanese, industrial policy is simply synonymous with good economic management.

Americans are divided in their views of Japan's industrial policy. Some see it as embracing two allegedly unfair Japanese trading practices. One charge is that the Japanese have deliberately manipulated the yen-dollar exchange rate in their favor. The other complaint is "targeting," as it is called, which selects certain industries and businesses, protects the domestic market, and tries to dominate the world market. The Japanese response is that the government gives some help to those high-tech industries that carry high risks and require heavy investments, especially in expensive research and development. Yet, as has been stated earlier, Japanese government spending on R & D is less than that of the United States. The *Keidanren* (Association of Industrial Organizations) has, in fact, urged the government to bring spending on R & D up to the level of Western nations.

The Japanese are accused of allocating resources to those sectors of the economy that can engender the greatest profits. This was true during the 1950s and 1960s, when the government deliberately fostered certain strategic heavy industries in order to create the basis for an industrial state. The four selected were electric power, shipbuilding, coal, and steel, and 83 percent of Japan Development Bank financing went to these industries. Ironically, two of those industries—

shipbuilding and coal—in the changed circumstances of the 1980s have been on the list of declining industries that MITI (the Ministry of International Trade and Industry) is helping to adjust to change. The other two faltering industries are textiles (long since a labor-intensive industry), which has passed to the "four little dragons" of the Pacific—Taiwan, South Korea, Hongkong, and Singapore—and petrochemicals.

Perhaps the most touted success, especially of MITI, in industrial policy is that related to integrated circuits. Since the mid-1970s, MITI encouraged research on sophisticated semiconductors called VSLI, or Very Large-scale Integrated Circuits. Five major semiconductor companies collaborated on the research from 1976 to 1980, with MITI assuming $123 million of the expense and the companies contributing $186 million. Initially American equipment was used, but the results were 1,000 patents, which in the end put Japan ahead in the production of the 64K RAM (a chip with a random access memory), enabling her to capture two-thirds of the world market. To deflate the coup of central planning, a trade association report recently revealed that Oki Electric, not part of the MITI-organized group, is the fastest growing 64K producer and was first to test the more advanced 256K chip. This kind of cooperative Japanese research would run up against anti-trust legislation in the United States and is the focus of American ire as a kind of Japanese government subsidy.

The role of MITI in directing Japanese industrial policy is a controversial one. There is no question that it is a powerful, competent, influential, and vital element in the Japanese governmental system. In prestige it ranks second only to the Ministry of Finance and ahead of the Ministry of Foreign Affairs. Its officials are brilliant, loyal, and indefatigable. Those who rise to the top can expect to perform the ritual called *amakudari* ("descent from heaven"), to assume top executive positions in Japan's leading industries, where their long ties with MITI will serve them and their company well. One must recognize that planning and targeting, whatever one may call the process, has played a significant part in Japan's climb to success. It has also not been the whole story, and MITI has made some dramatic mistakes.

Among MITI's failures was its rejection, in the early 1950s, of an application from a small radio company to buy transistor rights from Western Electric. A few years later MITI was persuaded to reverse its decision; the result, Sony. Also in the early postwar period MITI suggested that Japan's auto manufacturers combine to build a "people's car" of one design. The idea was soundly rejected by the Japanese automobile industry and no "people's car" ever saw the light of day.

In the matter of industrial policy, Americans are already attempting to find out what can be learned from the Japanese. A joint Japanese-American government committee on industrial policy has been set up. Numerous proposals, including a spate of bills introduced into the Congress, provide for various institutional and cooperative arrangements that might form an industrial policy for us. Critics have claimed that we do not have an industrial policy; that what exists is reactive, erratic, incoherent, protectionist, not conducive to fostering more competitive industry. It has been called "lemon socialism"; it bails out Lockheed and Chrysler when they get into trouble.

A group of congressmen, "Young Turks" (also called "Atari Democrats"), are promoting an industrial policy to aid declining industries, retrain displaced workers, bolster communities hit hard by changes in the economy, and, as in Japan, promote the "sunrise" high-tech industries. Among the Republicans, on the other hand, are those who depend on *laissez faire* ideology and eschew industrial policy.

The Republicans have apparently not been oblivious to the Democratic obsession with industrial policy. There are signs that the White House is considering setting up a presidential commission to study industrial competitiveness. A White House aide has been quoted as stating that the idea of industrial policy is not appropriate for the United States, and that Japan's success arose out of superior management and not government manipulation. Despite the vow to form a study commission, Reagan aides emphasize the dominant role of the marketplace. They have cited the machine tool and automobile industries to prove that it was not government that played the dominant role in the amazing rise of these industries. In fact, the whole concept of industrial policy and central planning runs against the basic philosophy of the Reagan administration.

As for Prime Minister Nakasone, he was very blunt when asked about foreign criticism of Japanese industrial policy. To the argument that European nations and the United States blamed Japan for endeavoring to develop and promote high technology through the fostering of private enterprises, Nakasone replied curtly, "This is not a problem which is of such a nature that it should be pointed out or criticized by foreign countries."

It is uncertain whether the rush to legislate, to form departments, committees, commissions, new banks, and government organs will meet successfully the challenge posed by Japan's industrial policy. It is true that the United States has not been overly adept in securing cooperation between government and business, or, because of anti-trust legislation, encouraging cooperative work within private industry to secure the benefits of central planning. More attention might be paid to modifying the structure of anti-trust legislation and, above all, tackling more vigorously the problems of our own economy. It is generally agreed that high interest rates and the yen-dollar exchange rate have been major causes of our trade difficulties with Japan. With signs that the economy is improving, perhaps some of the difficulties that have produced such emotional reactions will diminish. There is no magic solution, but perhaps the furor created by arguments and discussions over industrial policy has awakened Americans in government, business, and in the ordinary walks of life to the serious problems that characterize our relations with Japan. The deeper and more continuous the dialogue between Japanese and Americans, the more progress we can make.

There is no question, according to Ezra Vogel, a Harvard University expert on Japanese management, that in general there is a closer working relationship between government and business in Japan than in the United States. Compared to their American counterparts, the major ministries supervising economic activities are more concerned with improving Japanese economic capacities to compete in international markets and less concerned with regulating business and preventing unfair monopolistic practices. The Bank of Japan, for example, stands firmly behind the city banks, which in turn lend money to the largest Japanese corporations, and is ready to exert itself to prevent these companies from going bankrupt.

Compared with their American counterparts, Japanese businessmen meet more frequently to discuss problems of economic policy for the nation as a whole as well as specific programs and policies that would potentially benefit businesses of a particular kind. They are thus in a much better position to aggregate their interests and represent them to the Japanese government than are comparable American businesses. These differences become more significant as Japan and the United States face off in a growing trade confrontation that promises to increase in intensity in the years ahead.

CHAPTER 6

The "Japanese economic miracle" of the past twenty-five years has produced an export swell that has raised the standard of living of the average Japanese and the hackles of those Americans who have borne the brunt of the Japanese export offensive. The Japanese have not only exported finished goods to the United States; they have used some of their idle capital to invest in U.S. securities and to establish industrial enterprises for the production of automobiles, TV sets, and various other products in the United States. These efforts have been motivated not only by the opportunity for profits but also by the need to reduce the threat of U.S. protectionism. But they have not yet solved the dilemma of the imbalance between Japanese gross savings and the need to find outlets for these savings.

The question that demands resolution is how to achieve more equity in the trade relationship: What does the United States expect Japan to do and what does Japan expect the United States to do in seeking this goal?

What Japan most urgently needs is a change of philosophy, from narrow nationalism and mercantilism to a more genuine internationalism and liberalism. Japan is in a position today to

THE
UNITED STATES
RESPONDS

play the role of capital exporter that the United States played in the early postwar period and Great Britain in the nineteenth century. With its huge trade surplus and high domestic savings rate, Japan could not only improve its domestic infrastructure but could channel aid in larger amounts than heretofore to hard-pressed Third World countries that are short of capital and mired in unemployment and external debt.

But the habits of centuries change at a glacial pace and the Japanese will continue to save and accumulate large amounts of usable capital until the incentive to do so is diminished by changes in government policy. This may not happen soon, for while Japan is a wealthy nation, its citizens do not enjoy many of the amenities of wealth. Only 3 percent of Japanese communities have modern sewer systems, compared with 97 percent in Great Britain and 85 percent in the United States. Just 51 percent of Japanese roads were paved as of 1982, compared with 96.4 percent in Britain and 85 percent in the United States.

The Japanese consumer has many different products from which to choose and is daily reminded of the importance of purchasing more products from the United States to help alleviate Japan's large trade surplus. But such admonitions have not caught the imagination of the average Japanese, who is still attuned to the realities of the postwar era and the need to sacrifice personal comfort to the rebuilding of the nation. It is still a country where young boys wear shorts in the middle of winter to build up tolerance for cold. For many, national wealth has brought little sense of entitlement. With such ingrained habits predominating in Japanese society and acting to restrain government officials from conceding too much to American pressure, the likelihood of Japan adopting policies and changing philosophies that will nurture internationalism and liberalism and have a remedial effect on United States-Japan trade friction appears somewhat remote. Threats of protectionism will probably jar the Japanese government into modest concessions from time to time, but the kind of changes in the economic and financial structure essential to making a substantial dent in the trade surplus with the United States will undoubtedly run into domestic political and economic obstacles that will require cautious and at times ambivalent responses to the United States and Western Europe.

A good example of how the Japanese proclivity for thrift affects the trade problem is to note the rate of household savings. Savings continued to rise in 1985 despite slow growth in take-home income. A recent survey (January 1986) by the Bank of Japan revealed that nearly 96 percent of Japanese households have savings and that the average savings grew 6.5 percent in 1985 to $33,560. The ratio of savings to annual income reached nearly 16 percent (the ratio in the United States was 5.1 percent) for the fourth consecutive year. Fifty-nine percent of households have money on deposit at banks and post offices (Japanese invested over $350 billion in their postal savings system alone in 1984), while 17 percent have turned to life and casualty insurance and 12 percent to securities. Over 77 percent surveyed said they saved against illness and 43 percent said for their children's education.

According to Okita Saburo, a former foreign minister and a distinguished Japanese economist, the high Japanese savings rate is a heritage of an industrious but poor society. As Okita explained, a poor man who suddenly becomes rich cannot change his life-style overnight. By contrast, most Americans are living beyond their means. Yet change is urgently needed, and among the economic policies under discussion is the country's tax system. Many argue that the system encourages savings at the expense of investment. For example, only minor deductions for mortgage loans—a major expense for many Japanese families—are allowed, and there are less generous depreciation schedules and relatively higher corporate taxes than in many other countries. Most families save for the future rather than spend in the present. This has special significance for the economy in an era of an aging Japanese population.

Several private organizations as well as fiscal and monetary authorities are considering new policies to curb excessive capital outflow and redirect it to improvements in the domestic infrastructure. Domestic investment measures discussed include issuance of long-term bonds at attractive interest rates to raise capital for improvements in housing, school buildings, parks, public transportation, education (more scholarships and higher teacher salaries), nursing homes, and facilities for the aged, for pre-school children and for mental health care. About one trillion dollars of household savings are now earning tax-exempt interest. If the government were to tax these savings at about 20 percent, over $12 billion would be realized in revenue. This could discourage savings and speed expansion of the domestic economy.

But demands that the government adopt a so-called Keynesian posture to spend more in order to improve domestic livelihood have met with strong opposition from the prime minister and many others in the government. The prime minister's solution is to devise tax incentives and ease government regulations to encourage private sector investment and consumption. These efforts would probably be too modest and would likely have little effect on the overall trade issue with the United States.

The more critical the trade problem becomes, the more intense the dialogue. The United States trade deficit with Japan was $50 billion in 1985—up from $36.8 billion in 1984. By 1986 it was close to $60 billion and still rising. Charges and countercharges are flying across the Pacific over who is to blame, but until recently little of significance had been done to deal with the underlying causes. Most experts believe that there is blame on both sides. The huge Japanese surplus is attributable by many observers to an archaic Japanese financial system that was created during the period of underdevelopment and has produced booming capital exports and high savings rates, which have been channeled into export industries. Taken together with high productivity and selected tariff (duties on certain imports considered too competitive) and non-tariff barriers (excessive bureaucratic delays in passing imports through customs), the consequence for Japan has been a huge trade surplus.

The United States, on the other hand, has been shouldering the consequences of a large budget deficit. Tax laws which penalize rather than encourage savers have encouraged excessive consumption. The ultimate effect has been a growing trade deficit that has begun to weaken the dollar (the dollar lost almost 40 percent of its value vis-a-vis the yen in 1986–1987). So far, the increased value of the yen has had no appreciable effect on Japan's trade surplus with the United States. Americans continue to buy Japanese products because of their quality and the service rendered by Japanese companies.

Yet these rather logical explanations for the trade problem have had little impact on U.S. members of Congress who, rather than attacking the budget deficit, feel more comfortable in accusing Japan of closing its markets to American products. Fortunately the seriousness of the trade problem has prompted government leaders in both countries to take action in the areas of market access and exchange rates and capital markets (reducing financial barriers for investment in stocks and bonds) that hold out some promise for progress.

The Struggle for Market Access

The difficulties of market access for American companies are often attributed to the complex Japanese distribution system, which has several more layers than that of the United States and whose distributors may not always want to buy foreign products. Distributors place a premium on long-term relationships with suppliers, doing business with those who have faithfully performed their obligations in the past. It is sometimes difficult even for new Japanese companies to break into the Japanese market.

Fresh opportunities for foreign firms have not noticeably removed the special requirements—and frustrations—of doing business in Japan. The problem of breaking into an intimate community where loyalties and traditions run deep and where a better price alone will not disrupt the relationships that bind companies and clients always confronts "the new boys on the block." The rules of competition in the financial market, as in the commercial area, are often different from those accepted in the United States. Japanese financial firms appear to be more willing than American companies to suffer losses in order to establish market leadership.

Long-term relationships are even more difficult to cultivate for the foreigner who does not speak the Japanese language nor understand much about Japanese culture. While most Japanese businessmen in the United States speak English (they usually begin their study of English in middle school), few Americans study Japanese before arriving in Japan to work and only 7 percent subscribe to a Japanese newspaper. In addition to the cultural and linguistic gulf that Americans face in Japan, they often must deal with Japanese consumers who usually resist buying foreign products, in part because they believe that Japanese goods are superior. In several recent surveys, consumers said their reluctance stemmed from the generally high cost of foreign goods, uncertainty about follow-up service on the products, incomprehensible instructions, inappropriate size of products, and other details that do not fit Japanese conditions.

At their summit meeting in Los Angeles on January 2, 1985, President Ronald Reagan and Prime Minister Nakasone Yasuhiro decided to negotiate differences in their trade relations on the basis of MOSS (market-oriented, sector selective) and to include four major areas for discussion: telecommunications, computers and electronic equipment, lumber and paper products, and pharmaceutical products and medical equipment—sectors where the United States believes it has a competitive edge. Their decision was spurred by concern over rising protectionist sentiment in the Congress. On March 28, 1985, the Senate passed a resolution by a vote of ninety-two to zero condemning Japan's "unfair" trading practices and calling on President Reagan to retaliate by curbing Japanese imports. This resolution was followed by a Senate Finance Committee vote on April 2, 1985, giving President Reagan ninety days to obtain increased access for United States products in Japan or to take action under Section 301 of the Trade Act of 1974, which permits the president to initiate any action he desires against an unfair trading practice abroad. Many cases have been brought under this law, but the president has never taken a retaliatory action under its authority. Still, the threat of doing so has pried trade concessions from various countries. For example, South Korea signed a steel quota agreement after the United States warned that it might initiate a 301 case against the country's steelmakers. Argentina stopped discriminating against American air carriers after a 301 case was filed. President Reagan has not invoked Section 301 against Japan but has chosen instead to pursue negotiations through the MOSS mechanism.

But the Senate and House have continued beating the drums for protectionism, the latest move being a bill passed by both houses and presently (August 1987) in conference committee, which would level severe penalties on countries that have large trade surpluses with the United States. The legislation is aimed principally at Japan, and its enactment would have a damaging effect on U.S.-Japan economic relations. Although President Reagan has threatened to veto it in its present form, congressional pressure continues to build both on the Reagan administration and on Japanese officials in charge of trade policy with the United States. As a result, strong efforts have been undertaken by negotiators of both countries to achieve progress in the MOSS negotiations. Most satisfying to the American side has been the headway made over access to the Japanese telecommunications market, including international telephone and cable service.

Telecommunications

The fight over access to the Japanese telecommunications market, the second largest in the world after the United States, with estimates ranging from $5 billion to $7 billion, has been one of the bitterest in a long history of trade friction between Japan and the United States. A measure of its importance to U.S. companies is the belief by some analysts that the market may grow to $250 billion by the end of the century, as Japan strives to become the world's leading "information society."

In 1984, the United States had a telecommunications deficit with Japan of nearly $2 billion. This prompted the United States to step up demands for greater access to the telecommunications market, especially as the Japanese government had decided to end its control of the Nippon Telegraph and Telephone Company (NTT), formerly a government monopoly, and allow it to become a private company effective April 1, 1985. As a government monopoly, NTT had worked almost exclusively with favored Japanese suppliers to develop new generations of equipment and software. No significant business had gone to foreign companies. The lopsided nature of telecommunications trade between Japan and the United States and the privatization of NTT prompted the United States to urge Japan to renew negotiations over NTT access.

A major sticking point in the negotiations was the Japanese requirement that foreign companies wishing to offer value-added network services had to register in advance with the Ministry of Posts and Telecommunications. Some progress had been made on this issue as the first stage of MOSS negotiations ended in January 1986.

Another difficult issue involved products that use radio-wave pagers, mobile telephones, and two-way radios. Here too some progress was achieved: American companies would be able henceforth to enter certain radio-related businesses in Japan; required technical standards would be reduced; and the Japanese government agreed to accept test data supplied by foreign radio manufacturers for product certification.

The chief American negotiator estimated that telecommunication agreements so far have won about $2.5 billion in sales for American companies. Examples of new business for Americans include:

- The Hughes Communication Company sold NTT a $100 million communication satellite. NTT is now considering purchases of additional satellites from RCA and Ford Aerospace.

- The Digital Switch Corporation obtained a $20 million order from Daini Dendem, a company that runs leased lines over the Tokyo-Osaka grid.

- Paradyne has certified an ultra-high-speed modem to send data signals over telephone lines. This is one of a number of new equipment certifications that will increase the availability of American products in Japan

As the first round of MOSS negotiations concluded in January 1986, the chief U.S. MOSS negotiator said, "We are pleased with the results and I think you'd have to say we are in a parity situation." In a joint statement by Secretary of State George Shultz and Foreign Minister Abe Shintaro on January 10, 1986, both praised the MOSS system for resolving trade disputes and promised to utilize the system in the future.

Computer/Electronics

The computer/electronics sector has been an especially thorny issue for negotiators. In June 1985, the Semi Conductor Industry Association filed a complaint against the Japanese charging that American companies had been systematically excluded from the Japanese market. Japanese exports of IC chips to the United States, for example, have exceeded imports since 1981 and computer exports have surpassed imports since 1982. Overproduction of computer chips on both sides and U.S. charges of dumping by the Japanese have exacerbated the problem and have increasingly involved the U.S. Trade Representative's office in the dispute. The ongoing controversy is aggravating relations between the two countries and there appears to be no solution in sight.

Paper and Wood Products

United States-Japan negotiations over paper and wood products have produced more political difficulties for Japan's ruling Liberal Democratic party than probably any other sector of MOSS discussions. The current recession in the American lumber industry has been a principal motive for increasing pressure on the Japanese. The United States has so far failed to obtain Japanese agreement on the issue. Pressures on Prime Minister Nakasone, who has been a strong advocate of reduced tariffs on American plywood products, were under-lined during the negotiations when the Japanese side insisted on de-laying any reductions in duty on plywood until April 1988. Largely because of the Liberal Democratic party's traditional dependence on rural support, the Japanese forest products industry, after lobbying vigorously against lowering such tariffs, succeeded in achieving its goal, despite the prime minister's efforts.

Pharmaceuticals and Medical Equipment

The Japanese market for American medicine and medical equipment is considered promising by American officials and pharmaceutical companies, with estimates ranging as high as several billion dollars. Much to the disappointment of U.S. negotiators, however, the MOSS negotiations yielded very little progress in market penetration. The Japanese did agree to accept some foreign testing of medical equip-ment although with certain restrictions. Prior to this concession, American companies have had to replicate their tests in Japan. Japa-nese negotiators also indicated that foreign drug companies will henceforth be able to discuss their marketing problems with a key committee of the Ministry of Health and Welfare.

The progress that was achieved under MOSS did little to assuage the feelings of American companies, who have long complained that time-consuming approval procedures and Japanese refusal to accept foreign test data have blocked sales. While some regulations con-cerned with these complaints have been eased through MOSS dis-cussions, some American companies believe much more needs to be done. They see an aging Japanese population as a lucrative market for their products and are relying on MOSS negotiations to eliminate re-maining barriers. Analysts knowledgeable in the field believe it will be difficult to gain substantial Japanese concessions for the sale of medical equipment and pharmaceuticals in Japan but are optimistic that eventually a satisfactory agreement can be negotiated.

Increasing Domestic Demand

The United States has urged Japan to spur domestic economic growth as one way of dealing with the trade surplus. By stimulating such growth, Japanese goods and capital would be diverted to the domes-tic market and consumers would be encouraged to buy more foreign goods. After considerable prodding, Japan finally announced on

October 15, 1985, a package of measures to increase economic growth, including incentives to build more houses, expand consumer credit, increase local government works projects, and improve electricity and gas services. There would also be more holidays to give wage earners greater leisure-time spending opportunities. The Foreign Ministry estimated that the new program would increase imports by over $2 billion.

Economists were less sanguine. They noted that the government was still reluctant to embark on a program to expand domestic demand because of a large public debt that has produced successive austere national budgets. Also two traditional ways of stimulating growth were absent from the program—tax cuts and/or a substantial increase in central government spending. The Japanese government, Japanese analysts argued, is leery of adopting such measures because of fear of inflation and concern about adding to the public debt. Economists, diplomats and businessmen in Tokyo, both Japanese and American, believe the government's package will have too little effect on Japan's trade surplus to stem protectionist sentiment in the United States and Europe. While praising the program as a move in the right direction, they described it as too modest to accomplish the desired results.

Housing, they noted, is a case in point. For most Japanese, the cost and supply of housing is a pressing concern. Families cannot deduct the interest rates on their mortgages from taxes as they can in the United States; instead they are allotted a small tax credit. Japanese homes and apartments are smaller than those in the United States, chiefly because of the high cost of land. Over the past decade, in particular, land costs have risen at an alarming rate, especially in the great urban centers where most Japanese live. The average price of residential land in 1984 was $3 million an acre. Twenty Japanese homes could typically fit on a plot that size. Partly because of the high cost of land and of building homes, the Japanese construction industry has suffered over the past ten years.

The October 1985 government package contained a number of measures designed to encourage more housing construction and purchases, including raising the ceiling on government-subsidized loans while lowering their interest rates, and selling government-owned land to private companies that presumably would develop the properties. Most analysts believe, however, that these measures are inadequate to stimulate the housing market. One senior bank official I spoke with said that a major factor for improving housing construction would be the availability of cheaper land, not financing. In analyzing the government program, the Director General of the Economic Planning Agency said that the October 15, 1985 package may only achieve about 65 percent of its goal. He and other government officials conceded that there was much more to do before the domestic market would be sufficiently stimulated to put a dent in Japan's large trade surplus.

In order to give impetus to programs designed to stimulate the domestic market and in anticipation of a resurgence of protectionist sentiment in the United States, Prime Minister Nakasone appointed an advisory panel to develop recommendations to help solve the trade problem with the United States. In its report to Mr. Nakasone on April 7, 1986, the committee proposed a fundamental shift in Japan's economic priorities, in which the country would rely less on exports and more on imports and domestic consumption for growth. The recommendations were delivered to Mr. Nakasone in time for his meetings with President Reagan in Washington on April 13 and 14, 1986.

The new proposals were different from previous Japanese government efforts to reduce the deficit in that they were geared not to make it necessarily easier for foreigners to sell their products in Japan but rather to encourage domestic consumption. Included were actions to speed up public-works spending, the easing of regulations to promote private construction, and a combination of incentives and lower interest rates on certain government loans to small businesses and developers.

Some Washington officials were skeptical that Mr. Nakasone would be able to gain support in Japan for some of the more radical features of the program, namely encouraging the Japanese to save less and companies to pay higher wages to stimulate the domestic market. These officials also expressed some reservations about the prime minister's assertion that the trade deficit would start to decline in the fall of 1986. They cited, among other things, the reluctance of the Japanese bureaucracy to relax import controls, cultural preferences of the Japanese for Japanese products, and the huge cost advantage Japan's industry is reaping from lower oil prices.

On his return to Tokyo from his meetings with President Reagan, Mr. Nakasone was soundly criticized by leaders of the ruling Liberal

Democratic party for not consulting them about the new proposals before they were discussed with President Reagan. Bureaucrats were not pleased either. Austerity-minded officials of the Finance Ministry did not like the new tax incentives, and trade officials fretted about losing control over import regulations.

There were also basic economic questions. How readily can the Japanese economy be stimulated when Mr. Nakasone, mindful of large budget deficits, refused to allow extra funding for the new program? What about the millions of workers who, according to some estimates, might lose their jobs in the restructuring of the economy? And why should Japanese citizens save less when one reason they save is to protect themselves in their old age because social security remains inadequate?

There is finally the familiar question of how to make Japanese consumers more receptive to American products. The government has tried, for the most part unsuccessfully, to do so by slashing tariffs, adjusting quality standards, and making access easier for some American companies. However, progress has been slow and will probably continue to be so. American negotiators cannot forget that the deficit with Japan was $16.8 billion when Mr. Nakasone took office in November 1982. Since then his government has produced seven packages to ease trade tensions, yet the trade surplus had tripled to $49.7 billion by 1985.

Exchange Rates and Capital Markets

The United States embarked, as we have noted, on a two-pronged attack on the trade problem with Japan: pressing the Japanese for greater access to their markets for American products through the MOSS process and focusing on remedies to the undervalued yen vis-a-vis the dollar and greater opportunities for American participation in Japanese capital markets. The forum for dealing with the financial aspects of the trade problem has been the so-called Group of Five (United States, Japan, West Germany, France and Great Britain). This body has taken monetary actions to deal with the overvalued dollar and has served as an outlet for U.S. and Japanese negotiators to deal with various problems associated with greater access to Japanese capital markets. Most experts agree that a critical factor in reducing the Japanese trade surplus with the United States is to achieve greater balance in the yen/dollar exchange rate.

Yen/Dollar Exchange Rate

The Japanese political-economic system fosters inward-looking attitudes. It is incapable of selfless gestures, but it can react with alacrity once it is imbued with a pervasive sense of crisis. In the growing trade dispute with the United States, Japan cannot be expected to make significant adjustments in her economic policy until the entire economic establishment has been thoroughly instilled with the idea that there is a new reality to which it must adjust, just as it did to the reality created by OPEC (Organization of Petroleum Exporting Countries) in the early 1970s. No verbal threats serve this purpose because they have for many years proven quite empty.

The new reality is the persistent climb of the yen relative to the dollar, which means that American goods are less expensive in Japan and Japanese products are more expensive in the United States. Economists in Japan and the United States continue to believe that an overvalued dollar has been an important cause of the large Japanese trade surplus with the United States. It has reduced the cost of Japanese exported products and increased the price of American exports to foreign markets. Demands have steadily grown in the United States to correct the situation, and on September 22, 1985, the Group of Five agreed to coordinate their monetary policies with the objective of appreciating non-dollar currencies.

Notwithstanding these coordinated efforts, the United States continues to feel itself the victim of Japan's deep-rooted mercantilism. Running out of patience, the United States seems to have decided to hit Japan hard in an effort to produce a new reality in Japanese economic policy—reduction of exports and expansion of domestic demand. Mr. James Baker, the United States Treasury Secretary, thought he had attained such an agreement with Japanese Finance Minister Miyazawa Kiichi on October 31, 1986, when Mr. Miyazawa sought to stabilize the yen against the dollar and spur the domestic economy through a more generous budget. But on Christmas Eve the Japanese government submitted the least stimulative budget in decades. The U.S. government was disappointed and decided to use the only effective weapon available—allowing the dollar to fall further in value relative to the yen. By the summer of 1987, the exchange rate appears to have stabilized within the range of 135–145 yen to one dollar.

Analysts argue that the yen's appreciation should help eventually to reduce exports and thus increase Japan's dependence on domestic demand. While some progress has been made in export reduction, Japan's trade surplus with the United States continues to grow and there is presently little conclusive evidence that the yen's climb and Japanese domestic demand have appreciably increased. Some analysts claim there is little correlation between the trade deficit and the exchange rate. They reason that despite the fact that the increase in the United States overall trade deficit from $25 billion in 1980 to $108 billion in 1984 coincided with a substantial appreciation of the dollar, thus convincing many people that the strong dollar was largely to blame for the deficit, there were other factors that played a greater role.

A major contributor to the deficit was the collapse of U.S. exports to Latin America because of the debt crisis there. Another was the disparity in economic growth between the United States and other industrial nations in 1983 and 1984 (the United States grew by 10.8 percent in real terms compared with 3.8 percent in Western Europe and 9.3 percent in Japan) that affected primarily the import side of our trade balance, with the volume of U.S. imports surging by 26 percent in 1984 alone. The trade deficit is also the result of factors unrelated to the exchange rate, such as plant obsolescence, high labor costs, and rising trade barriers abroad. If the dollar's exchange rate were primarily responsible for the trade deficit, so the argument goes, it would have to be associated with a drop in import prices. But this did not happen. Non-oil import prices rose by 3.2 percent between 1980 and 1984. The import pull of the American economy was so strong that foreign exporters could maintain and even raise prices and still sell their products in the United States.

The Japanese government has been the most aggressive of the Group of Five in taking action to appreciate the value of the yen. But most analysts believe results will not show up in trade figures for another six to twelve months at the earliest. To implement the September 22, 1985 decision of the Five, the Bank of Japan has tightened credit conditions; this has resulted in higher yields on yen-denominated assets, thus increasing the demand for yen and raising the yen's value. The dilemma facing the Bank of Japan is that an increase in interest rates that raises the value of the yen could, if not carefully structured, cause a slowdown in domestic economic expansion, which could negate the Japanese government's efforts to stem protectionist sentiment in the United States and Western Europe. Already the rapid appreciation of the yen has caused serious financial difficulties for small Japanese export companies.

The yen's appreciation has affected not only small Japanese export companies, but large corporations as well. In December 1986, for example, about 7000 managers at the Matsushita Electric Industrial Company received envelopes stuffed not with cash but with coupons to be exchanged for Matsushita products. The last time company employees received part of their bonuses in products was right after World War II, when the company gave light bulbs—at the time its main product. The strong yen is exacting a toll on the giant electronics company as well as on other pillars of Japanese industry. In the first nine months of the Japanese fiscal year, which ends in March 1987, Matsushita's sales dropped 10 percent and its net income was off 31 percent. Hitachi's sales were off 4 percent and profits were down nearly 46 percent; and Sony reported that it lost nearly $2 million in the quarter ending October 31, 1986 and earnings for the fiscal year as a whole were down 42 percent.

Steel, shipbuilding, and automobile industries all suffered profit losses because of the appreciated yen. Manufacturing companies now find their goods less competitive abroad and must choose between raising the dollar prices or suffering declines in profits as they continue to bear the brunt of the yen's appreciation. The strong yen is thus forcing within the Japanese economy broad structural changes long sought by Japan's trading partners. The effects of these changes are just beginning to be felt: increases in overseas production, rapid declines in competitiveness for industries such as steel and shipbuilding, and cutbacks in employment.

Cut in the Discount Rate

In a policy shift tied to the rising yen, the Bank of Japan on January 29, 1986, lowered the basic discount rate, the interest charged by the central bank when it lends money to commercial banks, by five-tenths of a percentage point to 4.5 percent. For several weeks prior to the announcement, the bank had been under increasing pressure to lower the discount rate to stimulate the economy and head off what some Japanese economists predicted could be a severe economic slowdown. The pressure had come from Japan's trading partners, particularly from the United States, and was motivated by the huge surpluses Japan has carried in her trade relations with Western Europe and the United States.

The move by the central bank cast Japan in an unusual light—as the leader in a policy that, if followed by other nations, could eventually spur world economic growth and help ease the debt burden of developing countries. However, before the bank made its announcement, the Group of Five agreed to lower interest rates but could not agree on joint action to do so.

Most Japanese economists, while applauding the reduction in the discount rate, were pessimistic about its having the desired effect of stimulating domestic economic growth and thus helping to reduce trade friction with the United States. One high official of Sumitomo Bank estimated that a discount rate cut of 2 percent would be necessary to offset an economic slowdown. These economists also noted that the surging yen had not yet stemmed the outflow of Japanese capital to the American market, estimated at about $5 billion a month. They also observed that the yen's rise reflected a more fundamental economic factor—the falling price of oil. One analyst estimated that if oil prices settle at $21 a barrel (as of February 12, 1986, the price of crude had dropped to $18 a barrel), Japan's trade balance would improve by $7 billion. (Japan imports over 90 percent of its oil requirements).

Most Japanese economists' statements and editorial opinions expressed in the press were guarded in their view of the latest move by the central bank. Most conceded that without additional measures to stimulate demand the action would probably fall short of attaining the desired effect on the domestic economy. It would also, in their view, probably provoke further demands from the United States, thus adding to the turmoil in trade relations between the two countries. There is another aspect to the trade deficit and that is to promote faster economic growth in other industrial countries. This could mean more imports from the United States and from developing countries, thus contributing to easing the debt crisis and eventually to a resumption of U.S. exports to the area.

Culpability for the trade problem between the United States and Japan will very likely be established at some point, but for now the actions taken by the Group of Five to appreciate the value of the yen should eventually have a salutary effect on the United States-Japan balance of trade. As the yen continues to gain in value, the trend should act as a brake on Japanese exports. Yet bringing United States-Japan trade figures closer to some acceptable balance will require not only ongoing efforts by Japan but equally strong actions by the United States to reduce the huge budget deficit that has contributed so significantly to high interest rates, an overvalued dollar, and a resulting massive outflow of Japanese capital to the United States.

Capital Market Access

Capital market access and adjustment is the other major area that officials in the United States and Japan hope will yield some success in correcting the trade problem. The Japanese government has been slow to liberalize its money market, but it has recently taken actions that have spurred the process. In 1985, foreign banks were allowed in on Japan's fast-growing trust market, and foreign brokerage houses were granted membership in the Tokyo Stock Exchange. In addition, large-denominated deposit rates were liberalized, and there are plans to deregulate smaller savings accounts as well. Progress has also been marked by the introduction of new, high quality financial instruments and the promise of a freely functioning market in short-term government securities, mostly treasury bills.

Another major development has been the admittance of foreign credit institutions into areas other than commercial banking, most notably the trust business. In October 1985, three of nine American banks licensed to enter this new market started operations: Bankers Trust, Morgan Guaranty, and Chase Manhattan. Six foreign firms have been admitted to the Tokyo Stock Exchange for the first time, of which three were American companies: Merrill Lynch International Bank, Inc., Goldman Sachs International Corporation, and Morgan Stanley International Ltd. Participation in stock exchange activity promises millions of dollars in new brokerage fees for the six companies. Although easing of capital market conditions is doing much to assuage the feelings of American companies and government officials who have often complained about the difficulty of doing business in Japan, the problem of an expanding Japanese domestic market to absorb more American exports remains an elusive goal.

The new foreign presence on the exchange is the most visible symbol of the changes that have been occurring in Japanese financial markets. Driven in part by increases in private savings, the Japanese government has been easing the restrictions that have literally choked their markets and limited the ways in which individuals and institutions can invest their money. There are also indications that foreign commercial banks maintaining branch offices in Japan will soon be permitted to establish subsidiaries dealing in securities. Over the past eighteen months, regulations have been relaxed on foreign currency speculation and several new internationally traded securities have been created. As a result, Japanese capital has flowed abroad and a lively market in American Treasury bonds has started on the Tokyo Stock Exchange.

Another breakthrough in the Japanese capital market that should benefit American companies is the decision by the Finance Ministry in December 1985 to allow Japanese investments in foreign securities. Heretofore, the United States Treasury, through its sale of government bonds, has been the principal beneficiary of Japanese investment capital. Since December 1985, however, more than a dozen American companies, including McDonald's, Anheuser-Busch, and Honeywell, have raised over $2.5 billion from Japanese capital sources.

Tapping the Japanese capital market can mean sizeable interest rate savings for these American corporations. By first selling securities for yen and then converting them to dollars through a rather complicated transaction, the American corporate borrowers have usually saved about a quarter of a percentage point over a comparable issue done through normal channels. That translates into a saving of nearly $250,000 a year in interest expense on a bond issue worth $100 million. For years, the only real source of financing cheaper than Wall Street for large American corporations was the Euromarket, where issuers borrowed dollars or other currencies but not yen. Until recently, only a relatively small number of American corporations were able to raise yen in Japan through what are called "samurai bonds."

This new access to Japan's capital market stemmed from a May 1984 accord with the United States in which the Japanese agreed to permit selected companies to issue yen-denominated securities, principally in the Euromarket. For American corporations and other borrowers, the appeal of the Japanese market is the many billions of dollars worth of surplus funds Japanese institutions have to invest. As one American financial analyst put it, there is a staggering mass of private capital in Japan with no place to go.

The powerful yen has produced another unusual phenomenon, one that could affect future U.S.-Japan relations—surging Japanese investments in American capital and real estate markets. We will now look at this new Japanese challenge.

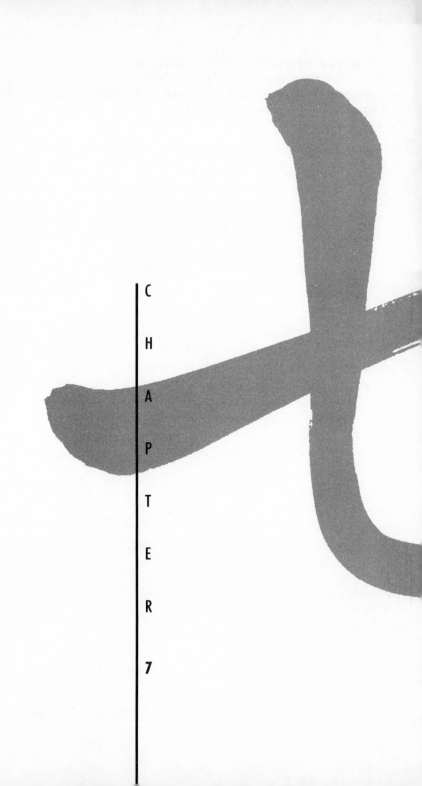

CHAPTER 7

From the surge of Japanese buying on Wall Street, to Fujitsu's attempts to buy Fairchild, to Mitsui Real Estate's purchase of the Exxon headquarters in New York City, a Japanese "investment wave" is breaking across the United States, bringing the possibility of greater cooperation but also the threat of further escalation of tensions.

For the United States, the new investments—and enhanced Japanese presence here—should be welcomed as a way to help ease the current trade controversy while fostering economic growth and the creation of new jobs. For example, in California alone, Japanese companies are the leading foreign employer and have added over 27,000 jobs for Americans during the last four years. Japanese firms in California employ nearly 77,610 people, up 56 percent from 1983. The three largest fields of employment are transportation equipment, electronics and electrical equipment, and banking. But these investments also have the potential for stirring up resentment.

For Japan, direct investment looks particularly attractive at a time when the dollar seems to have stabilized at a low level, thus insuring that acquisitions will not lose value in yen terms. This means that with the dollar level-

JAPAN'S SURGING U.S. INVESTMENTS

ing off at about 140 yen to one dollar, Japanese firms that have seen the yen appreciate to over 40 percent against the dollar can plan production and sales schedules with relative confidence that the powerful yen will remain strong and Japanese profit margins will remain stable.

There is some criticism in Japan about how her foreign investments are adversely affecting Japanese home industries, leading to a loss of jobs and rising unemployment. The Japanese Labor Ministry reported on July 7, 1987, that a structural change that is gradually forcing Japan's once unstoppable export-driven economy into greater reliance on domestic-led growth will affect millions of jobs in the next few years. About 11 percent of workers in the manufacturing sector, or about 2.2 million people, will shift into the service industries by 1993. Rising overseas investment by Japanese corporations, resulting in more factories abroad but fewer at home, could mean the loss of about 450,000 jobs in Japan over the next ten years.

Types of Investments

While the political effects of all this may be uncertain, the pace of Japanese investments is nevertheless accelerating rapidly, with portfolio investment leading the way. Net Japanese purchases of American stocks rose from $257 million in 1985 to $3.2 billion in 1986—and to $3.4 billion in just the first quarter of 1987. Japan also continues to fund a substantial part of the U.S. budget deficit through the purchase of Treasury notes. But the key development is direct investment, which has risen dramatically in recent years to a total of $23.4 billion in 1986—11.2 per cent of total foreign investment compared to just 2.1 percent in 1975. Fully 45 percent of Japan's direct foreign investment went to the United States in 1986.

So far, real estate has been the leading form of direct investment, with Japan recently overtaking Great Britain as the leading foreign landlord. Japanese investments should rise even more dramatically in 1987 as Japanese investors look for higher returns, and manufacturers seek relief from the export burdens of the expensive yen. Fearful of possible American protectionism, they also want to establish operations inside the United States.

There is also a new twist to Japanese investments in the United States—Japanese plants here are producing goods for the Japanese market. Thanks to the lower value of the dollar against the yen, some Japanese companies are finding it profitable to export to Japan from

Table 1

Trends in Japan's Direct Overseas Investment

Fiscal year	Number of investments	Value ($ million)	Change from previous year (%)
1951–73	9,504	10.267	—
1974	1,912	2.396	− 31.4
1975	1,591	3.280	37.0
1976	1,652	3.462	5.5
1977	1,761	2.806	− 18.9
1978	2,393	4.598	63.9
1979	2,694	4.995	8.6
1980	2,442	4.693	− 6.0
1981	2,563	8.932	90.3
1982	2,549	7.703	− 13.7
1983	2,754	8.145	5.7
1984	2,499	10.155	24.7
1985	2,613	12.217	20.3
1986	3,196	22.320	82.7
Total	40,123	105.969	—

Note: Numbers of investments indicate new investments only.
Source: Statistics on overseas direct investments (on an approval/notification basis) issued by the Japanese Ministry of Finance.

plants in the United States. So far only a trickle of products are moving back: Honda 1200-cubic centimeter motorcycles from Marysville, Ohio; Sony color television picture tubes from San Diego, California; Mitsubishi high power diodes from Youngswood, Pennsylvania; and Mitsubishi cellular mobile telephones from Braselton, Georgia, among others. But other products may follow. Honda, which also builds Accords and Civics in Marysville, says it now produces cars more cheaply in the United States than in Japan, and is weighing future made-in-America automotive exports to Japan. The company already uses Marysville instead of plants in Japan as the source of shipments to Taiwan, where some 2000 of its American-built cars have been sold. Sony and Mitsubishi are considering raising exports to Japan from their United States plants, while Mazda is interested in exporting cars to Japan from an assembly plant that it will complete this fall in Flat Rock, Michigan.

By themselves these moves are unlikely to do much in the near future to reduce the American trade deficit, yet the trend is another sign of how the 40 percent rise in the yen against the dollar in the last two years has altered the competitive landscape—a change that could mean higher American exports to Japan and significantly lower imports from Japan later in the decade. Exporting from the United States, or from anywhere outside Japan, also reflects the evolving strategy of Japanese corporations to set up global production. In taking their first step toward becoming true multinationals, with factories all over the world, Japanese corporations are doing almost exactly what American corporations did in the 1950s and 1960s. Fear of protectionism initially caused Japanese companies to establish manufacturing plants outside Japan. But the rising value of the yen has served as an additional strong incentive.

Since the mid-1970s, the Japanese have raised their direct investment abroad from $53.1 billion in March 1983 to $106 billion in March 1986. One-third of the total investment in 1986 was in the United States, and one-fifth of that was for construction or acquisition of production and assembly plants in the United States. Roughly $1 billion went into plants to make industrial and consumer electronics prod-

Table 2

Capital Flow in Japanese Investment in the U.S.
Capital inflows ($ million)

	Equity and intercompany account inflows	Reinvested earnings	Total	Currency valuation adjustments	Total
1977	424	163	587	−10	577
1978	770	217	987	7	994
1979	282	462	744	0	744
1980	92	639	732	0	732
1981	2,330	640	2,970	502	3,472
1982	1,850	126	1,977	3	1,980
1983	1,068	585	1,653	6	1,659
1984	3,073	1,301	4,374	334	4,708
1985	2,042	1,039	3,081	−8	3,073

Source: U.S. Dept. of Commerce, *Survey of Current Business*, various issues.

ucts and non-electric machinery, with most of the rest spread almost equally among automotive equipment, chemicals, and metals.

Even so, economists and other trade experts do not expect these new plants alone to reduce the United States trade deficit substantially. Japanese corporations have also invested heavily in Asia, Latin America, and Europe, they note, and many of these facilities will probably be used to export goods to the United States. In other words, exports to the United States from Japanese plants in these regions will probably replace the exports now coming from Japan. Since the start of the 1980s, manufacturing investment in Asia has slowed while that in North America and Western Europe has gained momentum. Investment in industrial nations has been prompted in part by the need to cope with trade friction.

Some might see the plans of Japanese companies to export to Japan from the United States as a sign that the attitude of Japanese consumers toward American goods in general has changed. But trade analysts caution against such an interpretation. All these plans mean is that Japanese consumers are willing to trust the quality of goods made by Japanese companies, wherever they may be manufactured. Convincing Japanese consumers that American companies can make high-quality merchandise is something that will take a long time. I'd compare it with the former reluctance of Americans to purchase Japanese goods because they thought they were cheap and shoddy, an attitude which took at least until the 1960s to change.

Some interesting statistics on trends in Japanese overseas investment and Japanese direct investment by country and area and can be found in Tables 1, 2, and 3 (please see pages 109, 110, 112–113).

Areas of Friction

Japanese investment has generally been welcomed in the United States. Various states and private businesses have competed for shares of the money. But there are beginning to be signs of what some Japanese now call "investment frictions." These prospective investment frictions stem from several factors, the first being the spillover from the trade problems. "Fair" trade and "competitiveness" are at the top of the political agenda, and when politicians talk about "competitiveness" they do not mean Britain or France. Even the appearance that Japan is freely buying up American properties with profits from an unfair trade system—whether true or not—could create an explosive political issue.

Table 3

Japanese Direct Overseas Investments by Country and Area

Fiscal year 1985

Country and Area	Cases	Amount*	% of total
U.S.A.	921	5,395	44.2
Canada	41	100	0.8
Subtotal (North America)	962	5,495	45.0
Panama	396	1,533	12.5
Brazil	22	314	2.6
Mexico	5	101	0.8
Peru	4	10	0.1
Bermuda	10	148	1.2
Bahamas	11	298	2.4
Caiman	8	132	1.1
Antilles	1	62	0.5
Chile	1	0	0.0
Argentina	2	8	0.1
Puerto Rico	—	—	—
Venezuela	2	2	0.0
Others	14	8	0.1
Subtotal (Central & South America)	476	2,616	21.4
Indonesia	62	408	3.3
Hong Kong	105	131	1.1
Singapore	110	339	2.8
Republic of Korea	75	134	1.1
Malaysia	60	79	0.6
Philippines	9	61	0.5
Taiwan	68	114	0.9
Thailand	51	48	0.4
China	118	100	0.8
Brunei	—	1	0.0
Others	27	20	0.2
Subtotal (Southeast & Northeast Asia)	685	1,435	11.7
Saudi Arabia, Kuwait	—	34	0.3
Iran	—	0	0.0
Saudi Arabia	7	4	0.0
United Arab Emirates	1	4	0.0
Others	2	3	0.0
Subtotal (Middle East)	10	45	0.4
U.K.	85	375	3.1
Netherlands	38	613	5.0
West Germany	48	172	1.4
Luxemburg	12	300	2.5
France	60	67	0.5
Belgium	10	84	0.7
Switzerland	15	60	0.5
Spain	8	91	0.7
Ireland	5	81	0.7
U.S.S.R.	—	—	—
Italy	11	32	0.3
Others	21	55	0.5
Subtotal (Europe)	313	1,930	15.8
Liberia	49	159	1.3
Zaire	—	—	—
Nigeria	—	—	—
Zambia	—	—	—
Others	6	13	0.1
Subtotal (Africa)	55	172	1.4
Australia	80	468	3.8
New Zealand	9	23	0.2
Papua New Guinea	7	1	0.0
Others	16	33	0.3
Subtotal (Southwest Pacific)	112	525	4.3
Total	2,613	12,217	100.0

*U.S. dollars in millions
Source: Japanese Ministry of Finance, 1986

	FY 1986			Cumulative total FY1951–FY1986	
Cases	Amount	% of total	Cases	Amount	% of total
1,232	10,165	45.5	13,757	35,455	33.5
52	276	1.2	766	1,951	1,8
1,284	10,441	46.8	14,523	37,406	35.3
373	2,401	10.8	2,747	8,841	8.3
30	270	1.2	1,326	4,857	4.6
5	226	1.0	243	1,556	1.5
—	—	—	96	696	0.7
1	16	0.1	84	617	0.6
18	792	3.5	71	1,247	1.2
32	930	4.2	92	1,279	1.2
2	66	0.3	36	376	0.4
2	2	0.0	60	182	0.2
7	17	0.1	118	176	0.2
1	0	0.0	39	141	0.1
6	4	0.0	89	136	0.1
13	13	0.1	479	269	0.3
490	4,737	21.2	5,480	20,373	19.2
46	250	1.1	1,427	8,673	8.2
163	502	2.2	2,568	3,433	3.2
85	302	1.4	1,860	2,571	2.4
111	436	2.0	1,393	2,118	2.0
70	158	0.7	1,009	1,283	1.2
9	21	0.1	633	913	0.9
178	291	1.3	1,631	1,051	1.0
58	124	0.6	1,111	884	0.8
85	226	1.0	296	513	0.5
1	1	0.0	30	103	0.1
13	16	0.1	391	243	0.2
819	2,327	10.4	12,349	21,790	20.6
—	41	0.2	4	1,309	1.2
—	—	—	108	1,003	0.9
1	0	0.0	98	361	0.3
1	1	0.0	42	233	0.2
2	2	0.0	69	110	0.1
4	44	0.2	321	3,016	2.8
142	984	4.4	1,190	4,125	3.9
60	651	2.9	354	2,337	2.2
59	210	0.9	817	1,552	1.5
16	1,092	4.9	99	2,308	2.2
52	152	0.7	742	970	0.9
7	50	0.2	249	793	0.7
7	91	0.4	220	753	0.7
15	86	0.4	163	601	0.6
4	72	0.3	62	332	0.3
1	1	0.0	7	194	0.2
18	23	0.1	156	203	0.2
23	57	0.3	265	303	0.3
404	3,469	15.5	4,324	14,471	13.7
42	289	1.3	679	2,744	2.6
—	—	—	56	282	0.3
1	0	0.0	89	157	0.1
—	—	—	17	142	0.1
7	20	0.1	319	353	0.3
50	309	1.4	1,160	3,678	3.5
104	881	3.9	1,313	4,502	4.2
15	93	0.4	228	354	0.3
4	1	0.0	190	200	0.2
22	17	0.1	235	178	0.2
145	992	4.4	1,966	5,234	4.9
3,196	22,320	100.0	40,123	105,970	100.0

Feelings could be rubbed raw in Japan as well, because of a major perception gap. Americans still tend to see an unbridled economic powerhouse called "Japan, Inc.," and there is little recognition of the turmoil and recession, of rising unemployment and fears of deindustrialization that the dollar's fall has created in Japan. For example, manufacturing costs have risen, export earnings have dropped, and the export volume has shrunk. The impact of the strong yen has also brought the unemployment rate up from 3 percent in April 1987 to a record 3.2 percent in May 1987. In addition, the number of overtime hours worked in the manufacturing sector has fallen substantially below last year's levels. The worsening employment situation threatens to curtail workers' incomes with unpredictable consequences for social cohesion and political stability.

The second friction concerns the fears of "foreign" control and manipulation that often accompany large and visible foreign investment. However, in this situation, Japanese investors can count on significant political allies. Besides businesses, their American partners will include local populations and mayors, governors and congressmen who see jobs being created and economic activity being stimulated in their districts. This factor differentiates the investment issue sharply from the trade problem. In the case of trade, the main constituency is consumers—the two-thirds of all Americans who, in a recent poll, said that they liked to buy Japanese products. Yet consumers compose too broad a category to carry political influence. Investment friction will be much better managed if United States business has equal treatment and opportunity to invest in Japan. If American exporters and investors are denied access to the Japanese economy, then Japanese investment in the United States will encounter more criticism and resistance.

Though many Japanese companies are reportedly pleased with the caliber of their American workforce, both sides agree that there are major differences in culture, outlook, and expectations, as well as attitudes toward work and the enterprise. How well the two sides adjust to each other over time will affect the overall climate for investment. This will be the case not only in times of start-up and normal operation but even more at times of stress—for instance, during unionization campaigns, affirmative action disputes, or recessions. Japanese companies will also need to be alert to the charge of "sticking together" and not doing business with American suppliers.

The investment wave marks a new era in U.S.-Japan relations, a logical result of shifting exchange rates and Japan's economic success. As we have noted, Japanese automobile companies are spearheading the advance. Electronics firms such as Sony, Toshiba, Hitachi, and Sanyo are also prominent in overseas investments, especially in the United States.

In the early years of foreign investments, Japanese firms moved toward commodity- and raw-material-producing countries to secure stable supplies for Japan's expanding industries. Investment in Asian countries dominated those early years and went through a rough patch in the 1970s, when some countries accused Japan of trying to take over the region economically. Since then the Japanese have trod a more wary path, but now the commodity-buying wave is over and the investment picture is beginning to change. The trend is now toward the industrial world. Japanese companies reportedly feel it is better to produce where the consumer is than to export.

Competition for Japanese Investments

State governments in the United States, as we have seen, are competing with each other for Japanese investments. For example, after considerable effort and hectic maneuvering, the state of Washington won a Japanese commitment for a $200 million integrated circuit plant in Vancouver, Washington. The new plant, a joint venture of Japan's Sharp Electronics and RCA Corporation, is expected to result eventually in a $1 billion investment and provide 1,000 jobs. Alaska was also able to induce Japanese companies to build two processing plants to make surimi, the basis for artificial crab meat.

The campaign to attract Japanese companies to the United States is gaining momentum. States are setting up offices in Japan to lure business and are sending trade missions there, often headed by the governor of the state, to extoll the state's economic virtues. Manufacturers are the prime target of job-hungry states. A study by the Japan Economic Institute showed that 479 Japanese-owned plants were in operation or under construction in the United States at the end of 1983, making everything from space-age ceramics to zippers, and providing more than 70,000 Americans with jobs. The number of plants has increased dramatically in the past two years. California has a large share of Japanese investments with 128 plants. Texas follows with thirty-five, New Jersey with twenty-seven, Georgia with twenty-five, Alaska and Pennsylvania with twenty-one each, and Illinois and Washington with twenty each.

Fueling this expansion of Japanese manufacturing facilities abroad has been a relaxation in Japanese monetary and fiscal policies. Japanese now have more freedom to invest money abroad through banks, securities companies, pension funds, and life insurance firms. Japanese companies have also benefited from Finance Ministry regulations that have loosened the hitherto tight rein exercised by the ministry in controlling overseas investments.

Is a Quid Pro Quo the Solution?

Despite these encouraging developments in United States-Japan trade relations, the massive trade deficit remains and is growing. Voices in the United States demanding a quid pro quo in trade are becoming more strident. What exactly do we want Japan to do to solve the problem and what is Japan asking the United States to do?

There is a temptation to place our trade relations with Japan on a basis of reciprocity but it is questionable whether such a policy would have the desired effect. Many argue that there is no reason why bilateral trade should be in balance. It is very likely that it will remain out of balance for the foreseeable future because of differences in the economic and social structure of the two countries. However, if bilateral trade gets too far out of balance, political pressures begin to build in the United States to protect threatened industries. But in the words of David Packard, Chairman of Hewlett Packard, in his testimony before the House Committee on Foreign Affairs on May 23, 1984, there is no deficit level in the United States-Japan balance of trade that is an absolute flashpoint. In 1983 the deficit was nearly $20 billion but was not considered disastrous. In 1985, the deficit approached $50 billion, and while still not injurious to the American economy as a whole, was greeted with deep concern in many parts of the country and prompted influential congressmen to call for sanctions against Japan and to demand a quid pro quo in the trade relationship.

The gap in trade may close over time as U.S. costs begin to come down and Japanese costs go up, but until then there will be continuing problems in United States-Japan trade relations that will have to be managed, that cannot be left to economic forces alone. Many theories on how to manage the problem have been put forth, some originating in the United States and others in Japan. For example, some American economists suggest that the best way for Japan to begin to defuse the trade controversy is to single out several specific industries and establish formal import quotas to be filled by imports from the United States. This, they argue, would have the advantage of relative simplicity and would avoid having the United States attempting to dictate every minute regulation.

A compelling case may also be made, so the argument goes, for Japan to put a tax on its exports to slow down penetration of foreign markets. Proceeds from the levy could then be used to accelerate Japan's growth without increasing its already huge budget deficit. There are also calls for reciprocity in the mutual reduction of tariffs. The list of demands from the United States is never-ending: Japan should restructure its economy, overhaul its financial system, allow unrestricted importation of American cigarettes, buy American automobiles even though the steering wheel is on the wrong side. The demands for Japanese reform read like a series of directives from General MacArthur's headquarters. But the occupation of Japan is over and the United States should be thinking about how to solve the trade problem in terms of an equal partnership and not in a *oyabun-kobun* (leader-follower) relationship of years gone by. Japan-bashing has become a popular sport in many quarters and is hurting the United States-Japan relationship.

The Japanese case against the United States is less complicated but just as compelling. They want the United States to reduce its huge budget deficit, which is affecting confidence in the American economy and the integrity of the dollar, and they want American companies to try harder to market their products in Japan. To deal effectively and justly with the trade problem, it would be better to dismiss the reciprocity or quid pro quo argument and concentrate instead on what is believed by many to be at the heart of the issue: Japan and the United States are, in effect, prisoners of their pasts.

Japan's huge trade surplus is generally believed to be caused by an antiquated financial system created during the period of underdevelopment. But in the 1980s, this same system is promoting Japanese exports and restraining domestic expansion. Fortunately, as we have noted, changes are beginning to take place in Japanese fiscal and monetary policy. For the United States, conditioned to being dominant in international trade and commerce, resentment of Japan's success has become an obsession that is blinding Americans to the realities of our mutual interests—maintaining peace and prosperity for Americans and Japanese. The United States as well as Japan must change its economic and fiscal policies along the lines already noted if the troubled alliance is to regain a level of tolerance and understanding that allows for vigorous and healthy economic relations.

I cannot deny that Japan's contributions to world peace have been far from adequate. Nor do I deny that its efforts on behalf of its own security and defense under the Japan-U.S. security system or its attempts to supplement and support the United States, the partner that has shared its nuclear umbrella, have not been all that they could have been.

Japan must steadfastly meet its duties and responsibilities within the collective security system to the degree that the Constitution and prevailing conditions permit. Fulfilling one's own responsibilities is an essential pre-condition for any collective security arrangement, and is fundamental to Japan's own security.

Japan should content itself with a non-nuclear defense of its territories, air and sea. By no means should it seek to become a major military power.

—*Yasuhiro Nakasone,*
May 2, 1982

F or the past decade Japan's defense policy has had essentially two faces, one for the Japanese public and one for the United States. For the Japanese public, nervous over military spending and a resurgence of militarism, government defense policies are carefully crafted to assuage its fears. For the United States, increasingly impatient over the slow growth in Japanese defense capabilities and struggling with a huge defense budget, Japan offers continual assurances of its intention to build up the Self Defense Forces and to assume responsibility for air and sea surveillance within 1000 miles of Japan. This dichotomy in defense policy has caused considerable misunderstanding between the two allies.

WHO IS DEFENDING JAPAN?

The Dilemma

T he United States and Japan view the world differently. For the Reagan administration, the communist threat, particularly from the Soviet Union, is the principal cause of global unrest and instability and the great challenge to freedom and democracy. The way to meet the challenge is by building economic and military strength. Japan, while acknowledging the danger posed by Russian military adventurism, is not convinced that her security is menaced by the USSR. Moreover, Japan's commitment to peaceful coexistence with her neighbors (Article 9 of the Japanese constitution renounces war as an instrument of national policy), the deep pacifist strains in Japanese society, the public's profound suspicion of resurgent militarism, and a national commitment to economic growth and a better life for the Japanese people, have all militated against dependence on military force to achieve national goals. The result has been to downplay the military establishment; emphasize the self-defense character of the army, navy, and air force; impose a ceiling on defense spending; and equivocate when replying to U.S. urgings for a speedup in her defense effort.

It is not altogether surprising that Japan and the United States have differing outlooks on security. Japan experienced total military defeat and occupation by foreign military forces for the first time in her history, convincing her to seek influence and gain international stature through other than military means. The United States, leading the free world's challenge to communism and drawing heavily on her own resources to build Western defenses, grows increasingly impatient with Japan for not devoting more energy and wherewithal to security. The onus lies especially heavy on Japan because of her enormous economic power. Her unwillingness to spend more than 1 percent of her Gross National Product on defense, despite her economic and financial muscle, has provoked a negative reaction in Washington. Japan presses to be treated as an equal partner, yet she has seen fit to make only a limited contribution to her own security. The United States has often been unsympathetic to Japanese explanations.

Yet the Japanese might be forgiven for wondering why, in light of the present American criticism of the uneven nature of defense responsibilities, the United States signed the U.S.-Japan Security Treaty in 1951 and the revised treaty in 1960, both of which provided for the United States to come to the defense of Japan in case of attack but placed no similar obligation on Japan. The defense relationship has lacked reciprocal commitments for over three decades, but only relatively recently has attention been drawn to the lopsided character of the treaty and to the lack of equity in defense burden-sharing. The principal reason is financial: As the U.S. defense burden becomes more expensive, Washington policymakers, looking for relief, press Japan for greater assistance. The growing Japanese trade surplus with the United States has also stimulated criticism from Washington.

This U.S. attitude has made Japanese leaders nervous, angry, and also uncertain about how to react to such criticism. American complaints have brought Japan face to face with the reality of her defense relationship with the United States: She must sooner or later allocate more money for the defense buildup program and make a greater effort to shoulder more of the general defense burden.

Defense Policy Considerations

As the occupation began, the United States was determined to demilitarize Japan. Japan's defense policy and the management of the defense establishment were therefore constrained within certain legal, political, and financial boundaries, the force and nature of which many foreigners do not understand. Japan has built and maintained its defense establishment through interpretation rather than through strict observation of these restraints. Nowhere is this more discernible than in the way the Japanese government defines its security policy under its constitution, a document written by the United States. The constitution has set the tone and direction for Japanese security and has been the major constraint in building the Self Defense Forces (SDF). Its clear message is peace: a Japan without offensive military forces, dedicated to the resolution of international disputes through peaceful means, wishing to live and let live in the international community, and seeking a better life for her people through economic progress rather than military aggrandizement.

This national policy is consistent in purpose and has been steadfastly pursued by all postwar Japanese governments. It has, however, fostered a climate of unreality and a stubborn reluctance to change in concert with an everchanging international environment. Working in such an atmosphere has made it difficult for the SDF and the Defense Agency (JDA) to carry out their responsibilities.

The Constitution: Article 9

Article 9 categorically states that the Japanese people "forever renounce war as a sovereign right" as well as the "threat or use of force as a means of settling international disputes." The latter clause, which during the Diet debates was inserted as an amendment by Ashida Hitoshi (later to become prime minister), permits Japan to consider the inherent right of self-defense as constitutional, since the objective of "self-defense" excludes the outlawed use of force to settle international disputes. Article 9 is the foremost legal constraint on Japan's defense program. Some Japanese would prefer a clearer statement of Japan's right to defend herself. With this in mind, in 1981 Japan's ruling Liberal Democratic party (LDP) reconvened the Research Council on the Constitution. The council published an interim report in mid-1982, but failed to reach a consensus on Article 9.

Prime Minister Nakasone has a long history of support for constitutional revision. He has confessed that when he met then Vice President Richard Nixon in Washington in September 1953, he urged that during a projected visit to Japan, Nixon express regrets that Americans had been overly involved in writing Japan's constitution. Whether prompted by his own original conviction or by Nakasone's suggestion, Nixon, on his visit to Tokyo in November 1953, created an international sensation by stating publicly that the constitution should be clearly revised to permit Japan to take positive steps in defense.

Nakasone wrote in the spring of 1982, before he became prime minister, that he has never changed his opinion on revision of the constitution, but that in the thirty-six years since its promulgation, the Japanese people had come to accept it, that it had come to be interpreted in a way compatible with the mores of Japanese society, and that while he would still like to see a constitution of Japan's own making, he would not want to rip Japanese society apart over the question.

That the constitution will become a serious political issue in elections to be held in the reasonably near future is unlikely. Constitutional interpretations, however, will continue to be debated. How far the interpretation of the constitution can be stretched until a consensus in the country develops to the degree that constitutional revision will become supportable and inevitable, providing for a more rapid and broader military buildup than is presently planned, remains to be seen.

The U.S.-Japan Mutual Security Treaty

While not a legal constraint on Japan's defense buildup, the U.S.-Japan Security Treaty has nevertheless played a central role in postwar Japanese security policy. The treaty has provided for Japan's protection against attack, especially nuclear attack, a consideration not covered by the Japanese constitution's Article 9. The treaty has also created a security environment in Japan of dependence on the United

States, which explains in part why Japan has been in no particular hurry to build up her defense forces.

During the period between the signing of the treaty in 1951 and its revision in 1960, several defects have been emphasized by Japanese critics. One was the lack of a clear commitment by the U.S. to come to the aid of Japan, by nuclear means if necessary; others were the open-ended nature of the treaty, the stipulation that American forces stationed in Japan might (if necessary) intervene in case of domestic riots or unrest; and the lack of restrictions on American operations from bases in Japan.

When the crisis over revision of the treaty erupted in 1960, the emphasis was on the issue of American troops and bases in Japan, their presence and operational activities, the danger of Japan's becoming embroiled in "America's wars," and the return of Okinawa to Japan. The one-sided nature of the treaty—failure to obligate Japan to come to the aid of the United States—was brought up in the U.S. Senate hearings on ratification. The new treaty provided for a review within ten years, and as 1970 approached, fears were endemic that another explosion might occur. In the meantime, however, the Nixon-Sato commitment of November 1969 to return Okinawa had been made and the furor over the bases had greatly subsided. The Japanese government decided on "automatic continuation" and the treaty ceased to be a serious, troublesome issue among the Japanese political parties.

The treaty has come to be accepted by the majority of the Japanese as a "fact of life," and as fear of a Soviet threat grows, support for it has increased. Recent public opinion polls show that 60 percent of the respondents support the present Japanese defense structure, consisting of the U.S.-Japan security system plus Japan's own defense efforts. Only 10 percent were against the security treaty, and only 6 percent rejected combined U.S.-Japan cooperative defense. In a separate poll, the strengthening of Japan's defense received 39 percent support while the status quo was favored by 37 percent. In general, the polls today (1987) reflect a greater percentage of support for the treaty as it stands.

This does not mean that opposition to the security treaty is dead in Japan. On March 15, 1983, just as a Diet committee had organized to propose amendment of the constitution, a separate group of fifty-eight Japanese legislators met to issue a call for adherence to what they called the "Committee of One Hundred Seeking a Revision of the Japan-U.S. Security Treaty." Others outside the Diet, representing industrial and academic circles, joined forces with the legislators to attack the "unilateral" nature of the present treaty, which requires the U.S. to come to the aid of Japan in an emergency with its "nuclear umbrella" but makes no provision for Japanese assistance to the United States. The opening statement of the group stressed three points: (1) that strengthened collective defense power is necessary; (2) that the unilateral nature of the treaty's obligations hurt the pride of the Japanese people; and (3) that the joint defense obligations of the U.S. and Japan should be set forth specifically because of the Soviet Union's threat to Japan's sea lanes. Every succeeding prime minister and each new Defense White Paper has emphasized the importance to Japan's defense of the U.S.-Japan security treaty.

The Three Non-Nuclear Principles

A policy constraint on the inclusion of nuclear weapons in Japan's military arsenal—nuclear weapons are considered offensive weapons and thus prohibited by law—is explicated in the three non-nuclear principles. These principles—that Japan will not possess, manufacture, or introduce nuclear weapons into Japanese territory—were first enunciated by Prime Minister Sato on December 11, 1967. At the time of the reversion to Japan in 1972 of Okinawa, on which (as provided in the agreement) no nuclear weapons were to be stationed, the Japanese House of Representatives passed a resolution reaffirming and continuing the observation of the three non-nuclear principles. In 1976 Japan ratified the Nuclear Non-Proliferation Treaty, thus assuming international as well as national obligations to remain a nonnuclear power.

While the Japanese public has consistently supported the maintenance of the three non-nuclear principles, doubts have arisen regarding the credibility of the third principle, the "introduction" of nuclear weapons into the country. This point was forcibly brought to national attention, becoming a media event, when in 1975 former American Admiral Gene Larroque declared that based on his naval experience, it was impossible that American warships armed with nuclear weapons would unload them before entering a Japanese port. The Japanese government spokesmen followed the line that Japan trusted the Americans to meet their obligations for "prior consultation," considered part of the security treaty, and therefore did not question the observance of the third principle. The Americans had long since established the rule that all government officials, when asked about the presence or location of nuclear weapons, should reply only: "I can neither confirm nor deny."

The heat was intensified when former Ambassador Edwin O. Reischauer, in an interview with a Japanese journalist in May 1981, remarked—in the context of a lengthy discussion of Japanese-American relations—that U.S. warships bearing nuclear weapons frequently visited Japanese ports and that it was time this fact be brought into the open. The Japanese government was highly embarrassed: To contradict a former U.S. ambassador who certainly must have known what had happened during the time he was in the embassy was difficult if not impossible. The government, however, fell back on its standard reply: that it trusted the U.S. government to live up to its obligations. The Americans, as always, were relieved from embarrassment by continuing to refuse either to confirm or deny.

The media barrage on the subject had, however, increased skepticism among the Japanese public. In a poll taken in 1981, 79 percent of those questioned did not believe the claim that nuclear weapons were *not* being brought into Japan. A question that received little attention and was deliberately left unexplained was, as so often happens in our relations with the Japanese, a matter of words. The English words "bring" and "introduce" have different connotations, the former suggesting a temporary action and the latter a more permanent placing. The Japanese word used for "introduce," in the case of the ban on "introduction" of nuclear weapons, is *mochi-komi*, which literally means—through its two Chinese characters—"to bring" and "put in." Thus when we say "introduce" and the Japanese say "*mochi-komi*," we both mean the bringing in and stationing of nuclear weapons at U.S. military installations, which, of course, is clearly prohibited under the third nuclear principle. On the other hand, it can be rationalized that the mere "bringing" of nuclear weapons in transit on ships or planes coming and going in and out of Japanese territory would not be "introduction" and therefore not subject to prohibition.

Since most Japanese believe that nuclear weapons are on board ships and planes that transit Japanese territory, some suggest that this be openly admitted. Such an admission would clarify an understanding between Japan and the United States and would remove the contradiction which some see in prohibiting the entry and exit of nuclear weapons in and out of the country to which we are extending nuclear protection.

Other Constraints on Defense Policy

Among the less well understood constraints on Japan's defense policy is her delicate financial situation. Even though Japan has become a major economic power maintaining a trade surplus with nearly all industrialized countries, especially the United States, she has been forced to live for several years within an austere national budget. Japan's cumulative budget deficit, as we have noted, is over $500 billion and approaching 45 percent of the GNP, a percentage level higher than the U.S. debt. This budget deficit has come about largely as a result of the sale of government bonds to finance government obligations. Her substantial trade surplus has been generated by the private sector of the economy. Government austerity policies have affected the defense budget which, over the past several years, has not included enough money to begin to remedy the shortage of ammunition, spare parts, and petroleum; or to correct the weaknesses in logistics and communication that encumber the military; or replace its obsolescent artillery, anti-tank weapons, and tanks that reduce the capability of the armed forces.

A further limitation on the defense buildup is the absence of a realistic blueprint for defense policy. The National Defense Program Outline (NDPO) or *taiko* was conceived in 1976 at a time of detente, when there was much wishful thinking about an era of peace between the Soviet Union and the United States. Japanese leaders believed they could devise a less ambitious defense program based on the presumed lessening of worldwide tensions and thus assuage the public's concern over defense spending. The NDPO, while outdated, continues to form the strategic guidelines for defense planning.

The vulnerability of the Defense Agency to bureaucratic infighting is another restraint on the defense buildup. In the tough bureaucratic world of Japanese politics, the JDA cannot compete with the powerful Finance Ministry, the Ministry of International Trade and Industry (MITI), and the Foreign Ministry for influence on defense policy. Constitutional and legal restrictions, as we have seen, are also a handicap to those advocating a more forceful defense program. An effort to remove Article 9 of the constitution or its reinterpretation would run the risk of losing what public consensus has been achieved within Japan for support of the Self Defense Forces.

Another constraint on the defense program is the concern in Japan about the reaction of Japan's neighbors to an ambitious defense buildup. While opinions differ in ASEAN countries and in China and Korea about Japanese rearmament, these countries have a common concern that Japan not become a regional military power. Paradoxically, Japan often plays on this sentiment to justify the modest nature of its own defense effort. A further restraint is the perception by the Japanese of the potential Soviet threat. While concern about growing Soviet military power in areas close to Japan, especially in the disputed Northern Islands, is increasing among the Japanese people, they are doubtful that the Russians will actually invade Japan, a belief reinforced by the presence of U.S. military forces in Japan. The Japanese do not fear the Soviet Union enough to support a large defense buildup.

Finally, there is the question of public opinion, which ranges from opposition to support for the status quo to advocacy of a major defense buildup. A large segment of the public, over 50 percent, favors only the minimum rearmament necessary to satisfy the United States. The gradualists, to be found mostly in the bureaucracy, in the business community, and in elements of the ruling Liberal Democratic Party, believe that Japan must step up the pace of rearmament in order to share the defense burden more equitably with the United States, and in so doing act in a manner befitting Japan's growing international prestige. At the extreme right is the group I think of as the Gaullists, pressing for a fully rearmed Japan, even one with nuclear capability. The Gaullist position finds little acceptance among the Japanese.

These constraints taken together form a substantial obstacle to the politicians and government officials charged with supervising and giving direction to Japan's defense buildup.

Institutional Framework for Defense

The Prime Minister's Office, which includes the National Security Council and the Defense Agency, and the Ministries of Finance, International Trade and Industry, and Foreign Affairs are the principal agencies within which government officials must function in developing defense policy. The prime minister, as commander-in-chief of the Self Defense Forces and head of the National Security Council, is the pivotal official in all matters of defense. Because of the diffusion of responsibility in the government leadership, however, in most cases he is more a chairman of the board than a leader whose decisions are final and authority unquestioned. Prime Minister Nakasone is often considered an exception to this general principle. However, while exerting strong leadership in defense matters, he has still at times had to bow to party leaders on critical decisions involving the defense buildup, especially defense spending.

His principal assistants in formulating Japan's defense policy are the chief cabinet secretary, top officials in the Defense Agency, the Finance Ministry, the Ministry of International Trade and Industry, and key associates in the ruling Liberal Democratic party. Much of the power in defense matters is wielded by the Finance Ministry, which controls the national budget, and the powerful internal bureaus in the Defense Agency, which set the policy for the operation of the Self Defense Forces.

Civilian Control

Civilian control has been a fundamental precept of postwar defense policy, but it was a new concept for the Japanese. Their first inkling of its power came with the firing of General Douglas MacArthur by President Harry Truman on April 11, 1951. The immediate reaction of Japanese leaders and the mass media was one of shock and dismay. General MacArthur, with his aloofness, his arrogance, and his supreme confidence, had filled a vacuum that Japan's defeat had created. The emperor was a figurehead respected by the people, but never considered a leader. The military, which had appropriated power and carried out conquests in China and Southeast Asia, all in the name of a "Holy War," "the New Order in East Asia," and "The Greater East Asia Co-prosperity Sphere," saw its senior officers and certain civilian leaders tried as war criminals, some executed.

MacArthur was the power, both literally and figuratively, and he carried out his role magnificently. Comments made after his dismissal suggested Japanese attitudes toward him. The President of the House of Counselors eulogized: "The sudden news was so shocking to me that I have not yet recovered from its effects." He referred to the "irrevocable loss and bewilderment . . . shared by the people of entire Japan." The two leading newspapers at the time, *Asahi* and *Mainichi*, in a joint editorial, expressed widespread feelings: "We feel as if we had lost a kind and loving father. His recall is the greatest shock since the end of the war."

The reactions to President Truman's dramatic and sudden action were bewilderment and astonishment that an unprepossessing civilian in Washington, even though president, could by one stroke of the pen fire a man who had come to represent to the Japanese people benign authority and power. This, it began to dawn on many Japanese, is "civilian control," and their discovery resulted in this principle becoming embedded in the new constitution and in the laws which later created the Self Defense Forces—a principle that not only U.S. occupation authorities insisted upon but one that was eagerly sought by the Japanese government. In their opinion, lack of civilian control of the Imperial Armed Forces had led to adventures in China, a major war, a disastrous defeat, and now occupation by a foreign army.

The Far Eastern Commission, an eleven-nation body established to recommend policy for the occupation but consistently ignored by General MacArthur, had the prescribed power to pass on "fundamental changes in the Japanese constitutional structure." On September 25, 1946, the commission reaffirmed a previous decision that "all Cabinet ministers should be civilians," and the draft constitution was amended to read, "The Prime Minister and other Ministers of State must be civilians." This remains as Article 66 of the present Japanese constitution.

The prime minister, like the president of the United States, is commander-in-chief of the armed forces. The head of the Japan Defense Agency (JDA), its director general, is also a civilian. The application of the principle of civilian control has sometimes produced friction between the uniformed personnel of the Self Defense Forces (SDF) and the civilian bureaucrats, most of whom—especially in the early history of the armed forces—were recruited from other ministries and agencies of the government, especially from the National Police Agency. A number of officers in the former Imperial Army and Navy found employment with the postwar defense establishment, but the passage of time has reduced their numbers to a handful.

The morale of members of the SDF has been adversely affected by the control of the civilians, and a sharp division between uniformed and non-uniformed personnel has been created. In the past, older officers, some of whom had had wartime experience, were brutally critical. One such unnamed officer was quoted in the *Asahi* newspaper some sixteen years ago as saying of the civilians: "They are petty functionaries who know nothing. They trample down the SDF by 'stamp' administration. At first they treated uniformed men as 'war criminals.'"

There is today a lingering antagonism toward the civilians in the JDA among the military officers. They complain that access to the prime minister by ranking officers is limited, and that policies are often determined without adequate consultation with the professional military. One factor that has acted to change these attitudes is the increasing importance of advanced defense technology. Specialists are essential, whether in or out of uniform, and their expertise is respected. A further explanation for the military's veiled animosity toward civilian superiors can be found in the circumstances surrounding the establishment of the Japan Defense Agency. Japanese civilians had never been responsible for military affairs and had little experience in dealing with the military. Therefore the first solution for establishing civilian control was to bring in police officials and bureaucrats from the old Home Ministry. Their strength was their administrative ability and experience. Their weakness was their ignorance of military affairs.

Another solution was to have selected officials from other government ministries such as Finance, International Trade and Industry, Health and Welfare, and Foreign Affairs take charge of procurement, the budget, liaison with foreign countries, and military medicine. This was the beginning of the dominance of officials drawn from these ministries for service in the internal bureaus (*naikyoku*) of the Defense Agency. These officials have generally remained in the JDA for only two or three years, after which they return to their parent ministries or retire. However, when occupying internal bureau positions, their loyalties are seldom questioned and they often aspire to become administrative vice minister, the highest career position in the JDA rather than return to their own agencies. Several officials from the Ministry of Finance have been appointed administrative vice minister.

The policy of civilian control of the military establishment has had the steady support of the government and the media—the latter in a rare display of agreement with the government on a defense issue—and firm public backing. Military officers sometimes chafe under these conditions and on occasion voice their frustrations, such as the time General Kurisu Hiroomi complained publicly that the military needed more authority. The prime minister promptly fired him. Despite the bureaucratic tug-of-war that goes on between military officers and civilian officials, a contest often shielded from public view, they do find common ground on defense policy, most notably as regards the defense budget. Military and civilian personnel work together in formulating the initial budget and have found that such cooperation facilitates later discussions with the Finance Ministry and members of the Liberal Democratic party. The military side acknowledges the primacy of civilian officials in the budget process and welcomes their support, especially if the concerned officials are from the Ministry of Finance or International Trade and Industry. Military officers believe such officials are often in a better position than JDA careerists to obtain results desired by the military services.

There is some sentiment among defense experts that the military services are slowly gaining more influence in defense policy, especially in the budget process, due to their greater in-depth knowledge of special military issues. The responsibility of the military services for the defense of Japan gives them a potentially powerful weapon to gain the essential resources necessary to carry out their missions. Yet, lack of strong political and bureaucratic support has often stymied their efforts.

Decisions that have Slowed Japan's Defense Buildup

Japan's defense expenditures since 1967 have never exceeded 1 percent of GNP, while United States spending on defense is approaching 8 percent of GNP. On November 5, 1976, Prime Minister Miki's cabinet decided to establish the ceiling of 1 percent of GNP for defense budgets. With continued rapid economic growth, defense expenditures were not expected to rise above that limit, and the maintenance of the limitation would appease a public wary of too much money going for military purposes. The 1 percent figure is not realistic in actuality since the Japanese defense budget does not cover, as do NATO figures, expenses of previous wars, including pensions. If calculated according to NATO standards, it is estimated that Japan's defense budget would already represent about 1.5 percent of GNP.

The Ceiling on Defense Expenditures of One Percent of GNP

U.S. criticism of Japan's "inadequate" defense outlays has been loud and clear for years. Its intensity has increased as the trade deficit has grown—a linkage that, while not realistic, has been inevitable. Since the Soviet invasion of Afghanistan and the growing alarm in the United States over the rapidity and extent of the Soviet military buildup in East Asia, voices have become more strident in urging Japan "to do more" in sharing the defense burden. The Japanese, with a different perception of the Soviet threat than that of most Americans, have retorted that their defense budget "sticks out" among other items, including education and welfare; that their budget is the eighth largest in the world in absolute figures; that their Self Defense Forces (SDF) are obtaining some of the most sophisticated weaponry in the world; that their public attitudes toward defense have become more supportive; and that the gradual increase planned for the future is not unworthy of a Japan with deep financial troubles and a populace which has had to be educated over a long period of time to the necessity of a self-defense system.

Congressmen are not persuaded by such arguments and have been severely critical of Japan, in large measure because of the unemployment figures in industrial cities—some of which are attributed to Japanese competition, especially in automobiles—but also because of the popularly accepted conviction that Japan is not "bearing its weight" in international affairs, particularly defense. Several resolutions have been introduced into Congress calling on Japan to increase its security contribution: One called on Japan to pay a "security tax" amounting to 2 percent of its GNP; another demanded that Japan spend no less than 1 percent of GNP on defense; a third asked Japan to "immediately increase its annual defense expenditures to the levels required for its forces to deploy fully by 1990 an effective self-defense capability, including the capability to carry out its policy, announced by the Prime Minister in May 1981, of defending its sea-lanes of communication." The latter resolution was passed by the Senate (the House of Representatives concurring) on December 20, 1982. Besides exerting psychological pressure on Japan to do more to build up her defenses, these resolutions accomplished little else of substance.

Prime Minister Nakasone, though supporting the 1 percent ceiling in principle, has stated that this limit was an artificial figure and that the standard must be what is needed for Japan's defense. The adequacy of a country's defense should not depend on a budget figure. The determining factors should be the roles and missions that need to be undertaken by Japan, the process of consultation and cooperation between the allies (Japan and the United States), which is now going on and should continue, and financial considerations.

During 1985 and 1986, the prime minister on many occasions voiced his concern that the 1 percent cap on defense spending was an obstacle to Japan's defense buildup and should be removed. He was finally able to convince the leaders of the LDP, and on January 24, 1987, the Cabinet formally decided to scrap the 1 percent policy, but hastily assured the public that defense spending would remain "in the area of 1 percent." This was a difficult decision for Mr. Nakasone, as the 1 percent limit had become a symbol of Japan's dedication to the spirit of Article 9 of the constitution. Some political analysts suggested that the leaders of the LDP had for some time recognized the need to change the 1 percent policy but had not wanted to take the political risks involved. They were comfortable with Nakasone being "out front" on the issue. The analysts also noted that the spectacular LDP election victory in July of 1986 gave Nakasone and his colleagues the confidence to take on the stubborn problem of "1 percent" with the expectation that the political fallout could be contained.

Nevertheless, the sudden abandonment of a policy that had seemed sacrosanct startled many Japanese and had immediate political consequences, touching off anti-Nakasone attacks from major opposition parties. There was talk of a possible opposition boycott of the Diet, an action that, if pursued for long, could undermine government hopes not only for defense but also for a far-reaching overhaul of the Japanese tax system. Despite the predictable harsh reaction of the opposition, no government or LDP leader has suggested that removal of the 1 percent ceiling means that Japan would stray far from its old policy of confining defense spending to less than 1 percent of GNP. Long before the present Cabinet decision, Japanese defense outlays had hovered close to 1 percent, and military spending for fiscal year 1987 of $22 billion will be only 1.004 percent of GNP.

Symbols, however, are important in Japan, and government leaders recognized that they had discarded a respected policy. But they also recognized that with the Japanese GNP increase remaining in the 3 to 4 percent range in recent years and with military spending obligations increasing, it would be virtually impossible for Japan to meet its stated military goals while at the same time staying under the 1 percent ceiling. Instead of a specific yearly ceiling, the Cabinet adopted a multiyear military program, 1986–1990, calling for $120 billion at an exchange rate of about 140 yen to 1 dollar, to be spent over a period of five years ending in March 1991; that is 1.04 percent of the projected GNP for five years.

Because of the sensitivity of the issue and Japan's concern about the reaction of its neighbors, the government instructed its ambassadors in China, South Korea, and ASEAN nations, to explain the new policy. Almost immediately after the Cabinet announcement, Japan was put on notice by the Chinese leader Deng Xiaoping that he was unhappy with the decision. Japanese leaders braced for similar criticisms.

The policy of abandoning the 1 percent ceiling on defense spending is characteristic of the step-by-step approach to change that often seems inconsequential to many foreigners, especially Americans. Yet it falls within a familiar pattern that can eventually lead to significant shifts in policy. Mr. Nakasone, a bold leader by Japanese standards and a long-time advocate of a stronger defense, appears to have viewed the breaching of the 1 percent barrier as the capstone to a series of changes he has pressed for since taking office. U.S. defense officials were predictably pleased with Mr. Nakasone's efforts. A closer look at the new policy, however, suggests that Mr. Nakasone is being very careful not to move too fast and too far and that the constraints discussed earlier still place a substantial brake on defense spending.

The National Defense Program Outline – NDPO (*taiko*)

The NDPO, created in 1976, has become institutionalized in the public mind as a deterrent to resurgent militarism and as an expression of the nation's desire for peace. As early as 1972, the Defense Agency was directed to establish limits on Japan's peacetime defense forces. Although some general principles on spending and force levels were established, they did not appease growing public anxiety over increases in defense spending. As discussions continued, the concept of "defense power during peacetime" gradually took shape. The brainchild of the late Kubo Takuya, an important official in the Defense Agency from 1970 to 1976, it centered on the belief that to equate the level of defense preparedness to the threat of attack need not be the basis of policy.

Established as official government policy on October 19, 1976, the NDPO marked a significant departure from previous defense programs, which had included one three-year plan (FY [fiscal year] 1958–1960) and three successive five-year plans (FY 1962–1966, 1967–1971, and 1972–1976). These had all stressed the importance of improving the fighting capabilities of the Self Defense Forces and preparing the military for any eventuality.

Conceptualizing a standard defense force capable of coping with limited and/or small scale aggression, the NDPO deliberately revised downward the buildup targets to be attained. It emphasized the modernization of weapons systems and equipment and the strengthening of the logistical support system but did not change the basic structure of the Self Defense Forces. Implicit in NDPO policy was the conviction that the most appropriate defense goal should be the maintenance of a full surveillance capability in peacetime and the ability to cope with small-scale aggression. The creators of the NDPO also foresaw the eventuality that U.S. forces would not be immediately available to defend Japan but assumed that these forces would at some point come to Japan's assistance, although no time frame was mentioned. The NDPO was not based, however, on a realistic assessment of the limitations likely to be imposed upon U.S. capabilities to defend Japan.

Despite these shortcomings, it is doubtful that the NDPO will undergo serious change in the foreseeable future. The National Defense Program Outline has been established policy for nearly ten years and it would be out of character for the government to change a major national policy, especially one so controversial, at an early date. Japanese policy has always emphasized consistency as a symbol of validity, and significant changes in policy direction are undertaken only on the pretext of positive public support.

The Mid-Term Planning Estimate
– MTPE (chugyo)

If the NDPO is the charter for Japanese defense policy, then the MTPE is the instrument that provides an incremental defense buildup plan to fulfill the broad objectives of the NDPO. Until September 18, 1985, when the MTPE became official government policy, it was merely an intradepartmental document of the Defense Agency to define the scope and costs of projects for the three military services and a mechanism to inform the government and the Diet of defense buildup plans. It was, in a sense, a "shopping list" for the three military services.

The new official five-year plan (1986–1990) revives the pre-1976 fixed five-year formula whereby the contents of a defense buildup plan are detailed and the estimated total expenditures required to implement the plan are specified in advance. This is a major departure from the post-1976 MTPE system that required planning on an annual basis. The new five-year plan, as we have noted, sets a guideline for defense spending for 1986–1990 at about $120 billion, or about 1.04

percent of estimated GNP for the period. Regardless of these guidelines, the defense budget must still be negotiated annually and there is no assurance that the ultimate spending goal of $120 billion will be met.

Under the new MTPE, priority will be given to improving air defense capability, modernizing Ground Self Defense Force divisions, attaining a better balance between front-line equipment and logistical support elements, adding new technological innovations to ships of the Maritime Self Defense Force, and increasing the effectiveness of intelligence gathering, reconnaissance, command and communication, sustainability and combat readiness.

The absence of a conceptual framework for these priorities in the new five-year plan and the question of whether there is a will on the part of the government and the Liberal Democratic party to provide the necessary resources are issues that worry some defense experts. The lack of a concept within which Japanese defense strategy can be formulated in precise terms, so that the public can better understand defense policy objectives and the need for increased funds to meet these objectives, is a major weakness of the new MTPE and could cause future budget headaches for the Defense Agency. Even if the NDPO and the MTPE were to be better understood by the public, there is no assurance that such understanding would translate into greater defense spending. Rather, given the past history of the defense budget process, it is unlikely that substantial increases in funding to meet some of the more ambitious goals of defense planners will be realized.

In order to support the objectives of the new MTPE and gain greater public acceptance of Japanese defense policy, the Defense Agency has organized a committee called "Operations Management Autonomous Inspection Committee." Among the committee's objectives are the production of recommendations for administrative reform of the Self Defense Forces that will lead to greater unification of command to deal with emergencies and to provide a conceptual framework for the new MTPE.

Pending Issues

The Strategic Defense Initiative (SDI). Evidence of close and fruitful military cooperation between the Self Defense Forces and American military units in Japan continues to grow. The recent agreement by Japan to share military technology with the United States is a further demonstration of the determination of the two countries to work together in the security field. This has not been accomplished without some fear by Japanese officials that a too close relationship might involve Japan in U.S. disputes with the Soviet Union or other Communist countries.

Nevertheless, cooperation is felt to be in the best interests of the two sides and has prompted the United States to invite Japan to join with Great Britain and West Germany in research on America's Strategic Defense Initiative program. When U.S. Defense Secretary Caspar W. Weinberger was visiting Tokyo on April 5, 1986, he again exhorted the Japanese to take part in the Reagan administration's space-based defense research, saying that Japan's technological prowess would enhance the program. Secretary Weinberger, aware that the issue of nuclear weaponry is a sensitive one in Japan, was careful not to pressure the Japanese.

In anticipation of an American request to join SDI research, the Japanese government dispatched a fifty-five-member delegation of government officials and industry executives to the United States in March 1986 to study the SDI program and make recommendations to Prime Minister Nakasone. The prime minister is thought to be a supporter of Japan's participation in SDI research but is meeting resistance within his own Liberal Democratic party, notably from Foreign Minister Abe Shintaro, who is a candidate to succeed Mr. Nakasone.

The official Japanese position is deliberately vague, merely stating that the government has an understanding of the United States space program. The prime minister is believed to support a program tailored after the West German model, which avoids government financing and restricts participation to private companies and research institutes. It is unclear what specific technologies the United States might seek from Japan, but likely prospects are Japanese advances in lasers, fiberoptics, and communications. Although some Japanese companies have expressed interest in the SDI program, they have not appeared as eager to participate as their European counterparts, who fear that they might fall too far behind in the high-technology race if they remain outside the program. Japanese industrialists also share this concern but appear more worried about whether they will be able to convert acquired military technology into marketable commercial products.

Despite some reluctance on the Japanese side to participate in SDI, Japanese government negotiators continued to meet with their U.S.

counterparts in Washington. An accord was finally signed on July 21, 1987, setting guidelines for participation of Japanese firms in the research phase of the space-based anti-ballistic missile defense program.

The 1000-Mile Sea-lane Defense Issue. In May 1981, Prime Minister Suzuki Zenko visited Washington and during the course of discussions with President Reagan indicated that Japan would consider undertaking, within the limits of the Japanese constitution, a defense of its territory, air and sea-lanes, to a distance of 1000 miles from the Japanese home islands. Since Mr. Suzuki gave his promise to President Reagan on the 1000-mile issue, the Japanese Defense Agency, while studying ways in which Japan could fulfill her responsibilities, has run up against the hard realities of an inadequate defense budget. The resources to undertake the defense of Japan's homeland up to 1000 miles are slowly being built up but progress has been slow and no target date has been set. Defense Agency officials are distressed over the slow pace; leading liberal democratic Diet members are skeptical and unsure of how the commitment to the United States can be carried out; and the Finance Ministry is unsympathetic to the Defense Agency's request for funds to purchase the equipment necessary to conduct the surveillance; and both the opposition in the Diet and the media are critical.

Richard Armitage, Assistant Secretary of Defense for International Security Affairs, addressing the Pacific and Asian Affairs Council in Honolulu on January 17, 1986, explained that defense of the sea-lanes by Japan up to 1000 miles of her boundaries does not call for stationing destroyers, anti-submarine patrol aircraft or air-to-air interceptors every so many miles between Tokyo and Guam and between Osaka and the Bashi Channel. Although these two approximately 1000-mile routes represent major arteries of Japanese commerce, the best defense, said Mr. Armitage, cannot and should not be reduced to a mechanical, tactical formula. The U.S., he stated, has never suggested such a plan to Japan.

Mr. Armitage emphasized that defense up to 1000 miles makes no sense for Japan if the United States is not working with Japan *inside* 1000 miles and is not defending Japan *outside* 1000 miles. Japan's complementary defense efforts with the United States inside 1000 miles constitute a meaningful, legitimate self-defense role and, through the U.S.-Japan division of defense responsibilities, provide critical defense to Japan, both near to and far from Tokyo in areas vital to Japan's livelihood. A consensus has yet to be formed in Japan on the 1000-mile issue and until this happens it is unlikely that demonstrable progress can be made.

Northeast Asia has enjoyed peace and stability for over forty years and much of the credit is due to the smooth functioning of the U.S.-Japan security relationship. The U.S.-Japan Treaty of Mutual Security and Cooperation is at the center of the relationship, and has served the common interests of both countries. For Japan it has meant protection from nuclear attack and for the United States the availability of forward military bases to help keep peace in the region. As the Soviet Union strengthens its military forces in the area, the security interests of the United States and Japan have taken on greater importance. Despite this growing Russian military power, however, Japan has been slow to develop strategic concepts for implementing defense programs to meet the Soviet challenge.

The Japanese tend to emphasize non-military aspects of security while the United States places greater weight on the military role. The American and Japanese perception of the threat and what should be done about it also differ, and this causes misunderstandings over the role each country should assume in the security relationship. Many Americans, for example, believe that the·United States is extending its commitment under the security treaty primarily for the sake of Japanese security, not American security. The Japanese, on the other hand, regard the treaty as primarily benefiting the United States by providing bases and thus putting Japan at risk in any U.S.-Soviet conflict.

The reality, however, is that the security relationship serves the interests of both countries. Japan needs a military force to protect itself not only from military attack but also from potential Soviet blackmail. Such a force does not yet exist, and to build up the Self Defense Forces to a level to accomplish these objectives would cost more than is currently appropriated in the defense budget and would also be politically unacceptable to the Japanese people and to Japan's neighbors. Yet defense cooperation between Japan and the United States continues to move forward at a pace that is helping to build the kind of national consensus in Japan that is a sine qua non for a more substantial military buildup and for greater sharing of the defense burden with the United States.

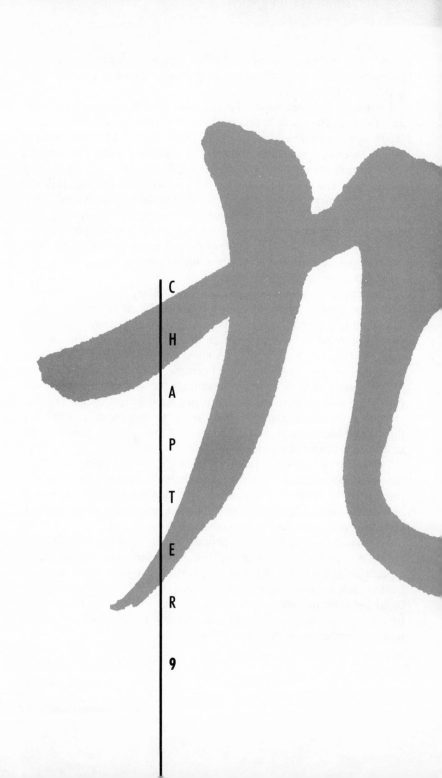

JAPAN'S NEIGHBORS: FRIENDS OR FOES?

While Japan and the United States have developed a highly competitive trade relationship that has caused growing tensions in the alliance, they have seldom disagreed over how to deal with Japan's neighbors—the Soviet Union, the People's Republic of China (PRC), and the Republic of Korea (ROK). Both countries have a common policy of promoting peace and stability in the area and have maintained a strong front in countering threats to peace.

The United States has military forces in the ROK and has deployed units of the Seventh Fleet in the East China Sea, while Japan has provided military bases and financial support of over $1 billion annually for U.S. forces in Japan. Strong U.S.-Japan cooperation has checked Soviet adventurism, provided a psychological backstop for China in her continuing problems with the Soviet Union, and brought a sort of modus vivendi to relations between North and South Korea. The U.S.-Japan relationship has thus set the pattern for both countries in their relations with Japan's neighbors.

Japan has been especially sensitive and responsive to post-World War II changes in her relations with the Soviet Union, the People's Republic of China, and the Republic of Korea, and to the way in which these changes affect her alliance with the United States. While there have been few disagreements between Japan and the United States on the common course to follow in relations with Japan's three neighbors, Japan has had her own special problems. These are to a large extent the legacy of her actions in China and Korea, and toward the USSR during World War II. A formal peace treaty has yet to be signed with the Soviet Union; the Chinese remain sensitive to current Japanese policies that appear to ignore the actions of Japanese military forces in China during the last war; and the Koreans continue to smart over what they consider the insensitivity of Japan, not only toward the ROK but also toward the 600,000 Koreans residing in Japan who still have only alien status. Although these are problems that only Japan can solve, both nations are aware of the continuing need to develop complementary policies—policies that take into full account the history and the present state of Japan's relations with its three neighbors.

The Soviet Union

For over one hundred years Japan and Russia have competed for influence and power in East Asia. They have eyed each other with suspicion, fought each other on the battlefield, and repeatedly failed to reach an accommodation on many of their serious differences. Relations for the most part have been stiff and formal, generally unfriendly and void of mutual trust and respect. Pragmatism not ideology has been the main feature of Russian policy toward Japan, while the Japanese have responded with wariness and concern over the foreign policy demands of their Eurasian neighbor.

The Russo-Japanese war over Korea in 1904-05, the breach of the Russo-Japanese Neutrality Pact by the Soviets with an attack on Japanese forces in Manchuria in the waning days of World War II, and intermittent skirmishes between the two antagonists in Mongolia, Siberia, and Manchuria are but a few examples of the troubled relations between these major Asian powers in the past century.

Things have changed little in the post-World War II era. No peace treaty has been signed; the Soviets continue to occupy four islands in the Southern Kurile chain—the Habomai group, Shikotan, Kunashiri and Etorofu—ceded to them at Yalta but claimed by Japan as historically Japanese territory; Japanese fishermen are arrested and held in Soviet jails for allegedly fishing in Russian waters; thousands of Japanese World War II POWs have disappeared in the Soviet Union; and crude attempts at political blackmail are often directed at

Japan's conservative leaders through unsubtle warnings of Japan's vulnerability to nuclear attack.

Practical and realistic when confronted with threats to their security, the Japanese have made a number of attempts since the end of World War II to reach some accommodation with the Soviets. The Russians, worried about their lagging economy, a rapprochement between Japan and China in the face of their own uncertain relations with China, and their inability to cause trouble for the U.S.-Japan relationship, have indicated at various times an interest in settling some of their differences with the Japanese—but on their terms. They want to share in Japan's technology and they want her help in exploiting the untapped resources of Siberia, and at the same time they want to discourage a resurgence of Japanese militarism.

While Japanese officials are deeply concerned over growing Soviet military strength in Northeast Asia and the power it gives the USSR to intimidate and influence, they maintain that Japan also holds a strong bargaining hand. They believe that Japan has what Moscow needs to rehabilitate its economy—capital and high technology. Meanwhile, Japan has diversified its energy sources over the last decade and no longer needs Soviet coal, oil, or gas as much as it once did. Japanese officials argue that if the Russians wish to focus on economic and financial issues, they must first be prepared to discuss the long-standing territorial problem.

A review of events in the turbulent relations between these two major powers since 1945 is instructive of how hope and disappointment, seasoned with mutual distrust and suspicion, can lead to alienation and failure. It also suggests how Russian inflexibility and unconcern for the feelings of the Japanese, mixed with growing Soviet military power in areas contiguous to Japan, have deepened distrust of Soviet motives and drawn the United States and Japan into a closer military and political partnership. Whether a more accommodating Soviet policy toward Japan under the new Soviet leader, Mikhail S. Gorbachev, will be forthcoming is questionable. A key testing point would be the territorial issue, and here Mr. Gorbachev's position has not deviated from that of his predecessors.

The Northern Territories

The territorial problem has stymied all efforts to negotiate differences between the two countries. Japanese officials acknowledge the reality of Japan's military weakness and of the ominous buildup of Russian forces in the area (according to the Japan Defense Agency, the contested northern islands are well fortified, especially Etorofu, with 10,000 Soviet ground troops, 3000 border guards and 40 MIG-23 fighter planes), and this has lent urgency to their wish to solve the problem of the disputed islands and restore normal relations with the USSR. So far, intransigence on both sides has discouraged a climate for productive negotiations.

In the history of the Northern Territories dispute, Japan has not questioned the right of the USSR to hold Southern Sakhalin and the Northern Kuriles, but has insisted that the four islands—Kunashiri, Etorofu, and Shikotan and the Habomai group which form the Southern Kuriles—historically have belonged to Japan. The Japanese have contended since 1955 that the Southern Kuriles are distinct from the rest of the Kurile chain and are Japanese territory. The issue is confused because the Japanese renounced all rights to the Kurile Islands in the San Francisco Peace Treaty, although the treaty failed to define what was meant by the term "Kurile Islands." Prime Minister Yoshida Shigeru insisted at the San Francisco conference that Russia in the past had never disputed Japanese ownership of the Southern Kuriles. The Yalta Agreement, however, stated that the Kurile Islands should be handed over to the Soviet Union.

The Japanese government weakened its own case by not being consistent in its claims to Kunashiri and Etorofu. At San Francisco, these two islands were not mentioned by Yoshida or John Foster Dulles, whereas Shikotan and the Habomai group were singled out as not being a part of the Kuriles and therefore rightfully Japanese. In 1951, the Japanese considered the Kuriles to include both the northern and southern group of islands and limited their claim to Shikotan and Habomai. But during negotiations with the Soviet Union in 1955 in London, the Japanese, who had indicated their willingness to accept the return of only the Habomai group and Shikotan, suddenly changed their policy and raised their demand for the Southern Kuriles as well. The Soviets, provoked by this turn in the talks, broke off negotiations.

Since 1955, the Japanese have consistently demanded the return of not only the Habomai group and Shikotan but Etorofu and Kunashiri in the Southern Kuriles as well. In subsequent discussions, the Japanese have studiously avoided mentioning the change in their position at the London talks in 1955. Since that time, negotiations with the Soviets have gotten nowhere, with each side showing no disposition to compromise. Despite the inertia that has settled over territorial negotiations, efforts to improve other aspects of USSR-Japan relations as well as to revive the stalled territorial talks have continued.

In the Japan-Soviet Joint Declaration of 1956, which restored diplomatic relations and set ground rules for the conclusion of a peace treaty, no specific mention was made of the territorial issue. The situation became more complicated in 1976 when the Soviets required Japanese citizens who wish to visit their ancestral graves on the four islands to have Japanese passports and to obtain Russian visas, whereas previously only identification documents were necessary for such visits. Japanese officials rejected Soviet conditions and grave visits were suspended.

Even though the Soviets are adamant on the territorial issue, they have made some attempts to improve relations with Japan. From time to time, Moscow has conducted what the Japanese refer to as "smiling diplomacy," and the Japanese have reacted by taking certain initiatives themselves. These joint efforts have resulted in visits by high-ranking officials to Moscow and Tokyo, cultural exchanges, and an aviation agreement that gave Japan the right to fly commercial aircraft across the Soviet Union with its own crew, the first nation to be allowed to do so.

Economic and Cultural Interests

High on the list of problems that have long been important in Russian-Japanese relations is fishing. The proximity of Soviet-Japanese territory has provoked controversy and confrontation, with many Japanese fishing boats seized by Soviet officials and fishermen jailed for intruding into Soviet waters. The annual fishing negotiation ritual has not been especially helpful in improving relations. The Russians have used the talks to gain concessions from Japan and as a reminder that the Japanese are dependent on Soviet goodwill to meet their fishing requirements. Negotiations are often protracted, tense, and contentious. The severity of Soviet demands is reportedly spurred not only by a depression in the Russian fishing industry but also by the Soviet desire to gain economic concessions from the Japanese.

With the assumption of leadership of the Soviet Union by Mikhail Gorbachev, economic and trade relations have shown some improvement. The two countries have signed trade and taxation agreements, upgraded the level of trade consultations, and reopened talks on scientific and technological cooperation, which Japan had suspended in the early 1980s to protest the imposition of martial law in Poland.

Japan has also been striving for a cultural agreement with the Soviet Union since 1958 but with little success. In June 1985 Japan proposed a draft agreement that would provide for a Japanese information and cultural center in Moscow, abolition of restrictions on the distribution of Japanese government publications in the Soviet Union, the creation of a cultural committee composed of officials in charge of cultural exchange in the two governments, and an expansion of the number of scientists that could visit each country. In four rounds of negotiations between June 1985 and January 1986, agreement was reached only on the creation of the cultural committee.

In May 1986, however, the USSR and Japan signed a new cultural agreement, which included a provision for cultural exchanges. The Soviets, for example, agreed to sponsor Japanese art exhibits and concerts in the Soviet Union, and the Japanese will sponsor Russian art exhibits and concerts in theirs. The two governments will encourage exchange visits of scholars and students. As part of the overall cultural accord, the Soviet government agreed to a long-standing Japanese request to open a Japanese public information office separate from its embassy in Moscow. Future negotiations with the USSR will determine when the office will be opened and what kind of information will be available to the Soviet public. The agreement also gave formal approval to a Soviet information office that was opened in Gotanda, Tokyo in 1957 without Japan's consent.

By broadening the issues to be negotiated with the Soviet Union to include cultural, economic, and trade subjects, Japan hopes to achieve a more favorable climate in which to tackle the tough problem of return of the four northern islands. There is a good deal of wishful thinking in Japan that the Soviets will finally agree to restore the islands to Japanese sovereignty. This has produced a sense of unreality in the Japanese government's territorial policy. Yet the key to Japan's strategy remains *ganbari*, or persistence, in seeking its objective and standing firm. Which side will "blink first" is pure conjecture. It is unlikely that Japan will give up the struggle, and it is equally improbable that the Soviets will finally accede to Japan's demands unless broader political and security developments occur to persuade the Soviets that it would be in their national interest to return the four islands to Japan.

Japan's participation in the Reagan administration's Strategic Defense Initiative (SDI) is another irritant in Japan-USSR relations.

Among the first things the Soviet foreign minister did upon his arrival in Tokyo on January 15, 1986 was to urge the Japanese not to take part in SDI. In his first meeting with the Japanese foreign minister, he said that although the Soviet Union did not expect Japan to criticize the SDI, he hoped that Japan would carefully consider its own national interests before coming to a decision. The Japanese foreign minister replied that Japan would make its own independent decision. (Japan signed an agreement with the United States on June 21, 1987, to participate in the SDI program.)

Whichever path Japan chooses to take in dealing with her defense buildup and in her relations with the United States, the People's Republic of China (PRC), and the Republic of Korea (ROK), she will still face a demanding Soviet Union. The USSR will seek her help in developing Siberia, continue to try to prevent a close alliance between Japan and the PRC, and pursue a policy of sowing friction, whenever possible, between Japan and the United States. The Soviets, however, appear resigned to close and continuing military relations between Japan and the United States and, in fact, seem relatively unperturbed, probably because they view the U.S.-Japan Security Treaty as insurance against the revival of Japanese militarism.

For the present, policy initiatives in Russo-Japanese relations appear to lie generally with the Soviet Union. The Soviets could put a bigger "smile" in their diplomacy, for example, by showing some flexibility on the Northern Territories question. It is unlikely, however, that they would presently feel it in their best interests to do so. Despite the antagonisms and deep suspicions that characterize Russo-Japanese relations, both nations wish to grow economically and to preserve their own socio-political systems; for these reasons alone, prospects for a broadening network of ties seem favorable.

Whatever the future holds for Russo-Japanese relations, history suggests that, at best, the relationship will be fraught with tension, hostility, and distrust. Russia will remain more foe than friend. The basic character of Russo-Japanese relations has convinced Japanese leaders and citizens that Japan's best interests lie in close relations with the United States and in harmonizing her policies with those of the United States on such issues as Afghanistan, arms control, and human rights. Japan will nevertheless be watchful and cautious in her relations with the USSR and endeavor to form and articulate foreign policies that will minimize antagonisms with the Soviet Union.

The People's Republic of China

China was the central issue between the United States and Japan in the 1930s, with differences over China leading ultimately to war between the two nations in 1941. China continued to be a problem for the U.S.-Japan relationship in the early postwar period. The United States insisted that Japan recognize the Chinese Nationalist Government on Taiwan as the legitimate government of China before the San Francisco Peace Treaty could be ratified by the United States. From then until the announcement of the visit to Peking of President Richard Nixon in July 1971, which caught the Japanese unawares and left a residue of bitterness, Japan had followed the U.S. lead in China policy.

Japan's China policy, like America's, had been locked to Taiwan. Japan's economic, political, and security interests in Taiwan were impossible to abandon. In spite of popular pressure to the contrary, the Japanese government, at least through 1970, showed no inclination to recognize the the People's Republic of China (PRC) on the mainland in place of Chiang Kai-shek's Republic of China on Taiwan, or to vote to seat the PRC in the United Nations if the resolution also called for the expulsion of Taiwan.

Japan and the United States had consulted closely on China policy. It was therefore upsetting to Japanese officials, as we have noted, to be told rather abruptly (Secretary of State Rogers telephoned Japanese Ambassador Ushiba Nobuhiko on July 15, 1971, to inform him that within thirty minutes President Nixon would announce his acceptance of Mao Tse-tung's invitation to visit Peking) that a fundamental shift in United States China policy had taken place. Shortly after the Nixon trip, the Japanese prime minister went to China, negotiated a treaty recognizing the PRC as the legal government of China, and in the process broke diplomatic relations with the Republic of China. Japan was henceforth to concentrate on economic and trade relations with the PRC.

Japan's bilateral relations with China have deep historical roots and are an amalgam of geopolitical and cultural considerations. It was in and over Korea that they first came into serious conflict in the Sino-Japanese war of 1894–95. This conflict had consequences of grave significance. Earlier struggles over Korea had involved only the immediate participants, but with European countries staking out their spheres of influence, particularly in China, Sino-Japanese relations became more complex. Russian expansionist aims in Manchuria and Korea confronted Japanese economic and strategic ambitions in Korea, leading to the Russo-Japanese war of 1904–1905. Japan's victory was followed by her colonization of Korea, which lasted from 1910 to 1945 and nurtured the ambitions of Japan's military leaders to expand Japan's influence on the China mainland. Korea thus became the continental base for Japanese moves into Manchuria in 1931 and into North China later.

The prolonged Sino-Japanese war of 1931–1945 and the Japanese military excesses in China (Nanking incident) were prominent factors both in shaping postwar Chinese attitudes toward Japan and in creating deep Japanese guilt over the treatment of Chinese citizens by Japanese military forces. The postwar period in Sino-Japanese relations began with contradictions: The attractiveness of the Chinese market and the wish to develop friendly relations with a nuclear power conflicted with the feeling that Chiang Kai-shek and the Nationalist Government in Formosa deserved special attention and help to compensate for the wrongs committed against the Chinese people by Japan.

Since neither the Communist nor Nationalist governments of China were at the San Francisco Peace Conference in September of 1951, Japan was ostensibly free to establish its own China policy. Yet pressure built in the U.S. Senate, as we have noted, to withhold approval of the San Francisco Peace Treaty unless Japan recognized the Nationalist Government of Chiang Kai-shek. Prime Minister Yoshida Shigeru, bending under this pressure, agreed to negotiate and sign a treaty of peace with the Chinese Nationalist Government. Japan thus became bound diplomatically and politically to the Nationalist Government in Taiwan. Her travail over dealing with "two Chinas" had begun and was to last until she broke relations with Taiwan and recognized Peking in 1972. (The United States normalized relations with the PRC in December 1978.)

While Japan's "China dilemma" began at the San Francisco Peace Conference, she was earlier alerted by the Treaty of Friendship, Alliance and Mutual Assistance between Communist China and the Soviet Union signed on February 14, 1950, that relations with these two Communist nations would be uncertain. The PRC and the USSR had pledged to come to each other's assistance in the event of an attack by Japan or any country collaborating with Japan in such an attack. The Japanese, then under U.S. occupation, hardly posed a threat to either Communist country, so it was reasonable to assume that the true target of the treaty was the United States. Japan was to view the collaboration of the PRC and the USSR as a potential threat to her own security and to political stability in the area and was therefore to synchronize her policies ever more closely with those of the United States.

Postwar China Policy

Meanwhile Japan was to trod a careful path in her postwar China policy. The main thrust of that policy was economic: to develop trade relations with Peking and Taipei. But even while Japan accented commerce, traditional feelings and emotions on both sides were to exert their pernicious influence. The reasons were varied, having cultural as well as political and economic relevance. Japanese attitudes toward the Chinese are complex and ambivalent. Most Japanese respect Chinese culture as the fountainhead of their own but disparage Chinese ability to command events in their own country and to deal effectively on the international scene. This Japanese attitude stems principally from contrasting their own rapid and disciplined modernization after the Meiji Restoration and their proven military superiority over the Chinese to over a hundred years of Chinese disorder and the slow pace of development.

Yet, if a Japanese desired to do business with China, he had to show a certain obeisance or "kowtow" to Chinese officials. This feeling of Chinese superiority vis-a-vis the Japanese stemmed from ages of cultural domination—the behavior of an aristocrat—and was flaunted at the Japanese who reluctantly accepted the "kowtow" requirement in the interest of selling their products to China. But it grated, and they often resorted to a patronizing attitude toward the aged patrician who did not appear able to bring order out of political and social chaos. The old aristocrat didn't seem to mind. He felt secure in his numbers, in the breadth of his territory, in his nuclear capability, and in his historical predominance in Asia.

The built-in friction and tension in the attitudes of Chinese and Japanese toward each other, however, has not made for comfortable relations. Competitiveness and rivalry for predominance in Asian affairs has been papered over when it has suited both parties to do so, but it has underlined their bilateral relations from the beginning. Mixed with these strong adversarial feelings, however, is a degree of pragmatism that has allowed two disparate political and economic systems to trade with each other and to adjust to changes in the power balance in East Asia.

Japan, in adopting her "two China policy" during the 1950s, was able to develop trade with both Chinas but not without difficulty. The antagonisms between Peking and Taipei caused Japan to pursue a delicate balancing act, trying to expand trade with China while keeping stable diplomatic relations with Taiwan. Setbacks in 1958, when China suddenly stopped trade, and again in 1963 when Taiwan almost broke diplomatic relations, were overcome with patience, stoicism, and a determination not to allow political considerations to affect Japan's trade policies. This strategy of the "separation of politics and economics," which Japan proclaimed as the underlying philosophy of her economic policy, was attacked repeatedly by China. Peking stressed that trade and politics were inseparable.

In the spring of 1970, Premier Chou En-lai announced four principles which were to govern China's trade with Japan. The gist of these was that China would not trade with firms which (1) carried on trade with South Korea and Taiwan, (2) invested in South Korea and Taiwan, (3) exported weapons for American use in Vietnam, Laos, and Cambodia, and (4) were affiliated with American firms in Japan in joint ventures or as subsidiaries. Attacks on the alleged revival of Japanese militarism and charges that Japan intended to create two Chinas accompanied the Chou announcement and grew in stridency as the months passed.

In late 1971, however, the torrent of abusive propaganda from Peking began to subside. Chinese Communist leaders appeared to feel that the upcoming visit of President Nixon was evidence that Washington did not intend to promote Japanese militarism. They also hoped for an agreement to normalize their relations with Japan. As events turned out, the Japanese prime minister did visit Peking in late 1972, reached an understanding that included recognition of Peking as the sole legitimate government of China; severance of diplomatic relations with Taiwan and establishment of diplomatic relations with China; Japan's adherence to the provision of the Potsdam Agreement concerning the return of Taiwan to China; and Japan's acceptance of the view that the 1952 peace treaty with Taiwan was no longer in effect.

Economic Relations

The period of the mid-1970s to the mid-1980s saw both countries concentrating on economic development. It was a period when China, under the leadership of Deng Xiaoping, embarked on an ambitious program of modernization, and Japan concentrated on expanding her export markets. It also saw the Sino-Japanese relationship reach another important plateau with the signing of the Sino-Japanese Treaty of Peace and Friendship in August of 1978. Since China's economy began to accelerate under Deng's new program, there has been much talk of a "China boom" in Japan as economic exchanges through trade and investment have become active. The impetus behind this development is a fast-growing Chinese economy that recorded a growth of 12 percent in 1984. Two-way trade between Japan and China in 1984 totalled $13.2 billion. The expansion has continued since the beginning of 1985, with Japanese exports showing a steep increase, spearheaded by consumer electrical appliances. Machinery and steel accounted for 40 percent, and when chemicals were included, the shares of the three heavy industries rose to about 90 percent.

The rapid pace of Sino-Japanese trade is beginning, however, to cause problems. One is the trade imbalance. Japan has run surpluses every year except 1981–82, when China strengthened import curbs under an economic adjustment that called for scaling down major industrial projects, reducing the budget deficit, stabilizing prices, emphasizing agriculture and light industry, and conserving energy. Japan's surplus again began to swell in 1984 and this trend continues, fueled mainly by a surge in Chinese imports.

The "China boom" will not go away. For centuries, China's size and population have beckoned traders. Textile manufacturers in nineteenth-century England dreamed of making their fortune by supplying every Chinese with just one shirt, and American merchants dazzled by similar visions helped force China's door open. Japan has now heeded the call. The dreams are now of color television sets and refrigerators. As one Japanese businessman calculates, if there are 230 million households in China, and if six and one-half million color television sets are sold in a year, it would still leave 95 percent of the market unsupplied. Encouraged by China's new trade policies and blocked by protectionist actions in Europe and the threat of such actions in the United States, the Japanese businessman has turned increasingly to the Chinese market. His country is now China's largest trading partner.

The attraction of the huge China market for the Japanese entrepreneur is sometimes offset by the hard realities of dealing with China. The Chinese have proven tough negotiators, playing manufacturers against each other to receive rock bottom bids. Joint ventures have often been restricted to relatively short periods, and prices for factory sites have been inflated by Japanese standards. Workers with little training in quality control or Japanese standards of production have posed management problems for Japanese manufacturers. As a high Japanese government official put it, many Japanese businessmen have inflated expectations and grow discouraged when they find that Chinese conduct business in very different ways. Despite current trading difficulties, which many Japanese businessmen consider temporary, large and long-term investments in the Chinese market are being made by major Japanese companies. In addition to direct investments, Japanese companies are vigorously promoting China trade as middlemen between China and third countries.

Other Problems

While trade usually takes center stage in contemporary Japan-China relations, there are other aspects of the relationship that require attention and find their wellsprings in historical rivalries and attitudinal differences. I have already described the superiority/inferiority syndrome that influences the behavior of Japanese and Chinese toward each other and the military excesses committed by Japanese military forces against the Chinese population during the last Sino-Japanese war, which left a heavy imprint on relations and evoked strong Chinese reaction to presumed Japanese insensitivity to wartime crimes.

Evidence of Japanese military brutality and a probable calculated effort by the Chinese to use that evidence to extract trade and other concessions from the Japanese government appeared to be the principal motives behind Chinese reaction to the Japanese prime minister's official visit to Yasukuni Shrine in Tokyo on August 15, 1985, to pay homage to Japan's war dead. That the leader of the Japanese government would pay his respects to soldiers who committed crimes against the Chinese people presented an opportunity to exert leverage on Japan that was too tempting to resist. Whether fabricated or genuine (probably a little of both), Chinese outrage was expressed by strong official disapproval and student street demonstrations.

Japanese reaction to all this was to be cautious and quiet. Yasukuni Shrine, near the Imperial Palace grounds in Tokyo, honors the spirit of nearly two and a half million Japanese soldiers who died for their country in the last century. Among those whose souls rest there, however, are convicted war criminals like Japan's prime minister at the time of Pearl Harbor, General Tojo Hideki. The shrine embodies much of the prewar sentiment of *bushido*, or the spirit of the warrior, and Japan's leaders have been careful to avoid any actions involving the shrine that could arouse the suspicion of Japan's neighbors that Japan was on the road back to militarism.

The controversy, although rooted in symbolism, demonstrates the extent to which Japan's wartime aggression shadows its present foreign relations. Other Asian nations continue to look warily for signs of resurgent Japanese militarism, and Tokyo often reacts with open edginess every time the issue arises. Japanese officials are especially uneasy when complaints come from China, because Japan owes so much of its cultural heritage to China. This Chinese sensitivity resembles that shown in 1982 when China denounced what it claimed were distortions in Japanese textbook accounts of Japan's wartime occupation of Manchuria, and again in July 1986, when similar criticisms were leveled at the Japanese Education Ministry for approving a senior high-school textbook that the Chinese claimed was full of erroneous facts concerning Japan's invasion of China in World War II. The Yasukuni Shrine, trade, and textbooks, if not handled diplomatically by Japan (and they appear to have been so far), could serve to ignite frictions in Sino-Japanese relations, which for the Chinese would hold opportunities and for the Japanese, headaches.

A final means of assessing relations between China and Japan is to consider the forces at work in shaping the triangular relationship of Japan, China, and the Soviet Union. Japan gains from the Sino-Soviet confrontation. As China's fear of the USSR increases, she is more prone to seek policy accommodations with Japan. Conversely, as China and Japan appear to move closer together, the Soviets become worried and begin to explore ways of negotiating with Japan on economic and commercial issues, especially those involving the development of Siberian resources. Thus Japan has greater flexibility and maneuvering room in her relations with her giant Communist neighbors. Both the Soviet Union and China are presently satisfied with Japan's security ties with the United States. Each would rather see Japan's security link with the United States maintained than have Japan join in a defense relationship with the other.

Sino-Japanese relations will ultimately be influenced not only by the Sino-Soviet confrontation and relations among the United States, China, and the USSR, but also by the state of relations between Japan and the United States. The more robust the relationship between

Japan and the United States, the more leverage Japan will have in negotiating with China and the Soviet Union.

It appears likely that conflicts of interest with China will become more pronounced as Japan's economic influence expands further and she attempts to cultivate political and economic ties with ASEAN countries. Should this happen, Japan's relations with the United States will take on added importance. The greater Japan's confidence that she has the respect and support of the United States and can rely on the U.S. commitment under the U.S.-Japan Security Treaty, the less she will be inclined to bend to pressures from China or the Soviet Union.

The Republic of Korea (ROK)

Japan and the United States have common interests in Korea— peace and political stability on the Korean peninsula. Anxiety over a hostile Korea has long been a staple of the Japanese psyche. President Jimmy Carter's proposal to withdraw American military forces from South Korea during his campaign for the presidency, for example, evoked expressions of deep concern from Japanese leaders and the press.

Japan-Korea relations are formal and outwardly civil, but there is evidence of growing economic tensions and continuing Korean sensitivity to Japanese discrimination against Koreans in Japan and the imperious attitude exhibited by some Japanese leaders toward the ROK. These bilateral frictions have had little serious impact on basic U.S.-Japan relations. American military forces in South Korea, however, are dependent on rear echelon support in Japan, and political and economic tensions between these two Pacific allies of the United States could adversely affect the U.S. military presence in the area. Strained relations between Japan and South Korea could also tempt North Korea to "test the waters" on the peninsula, resulting in the destabilization of the tenuous peace that has existed between North and South Korea since the cessation of hostilities in 1953. Both the United States and Japan recognize the volatility in North-South Korea relations and are continually alert to danger signs.

The ROK must not only live with the reality of a divided Korean peninsula, a hostile North Korea, a postwar civil conflict that devastated both North and South Korea, but also memories of a powerful and arrogant prewar Japan that subjugated Korea and embittered the Korean people. It was Japan's colonial rule, as we have described it, and the events that preceded it that established the basic Korean attitude toward Japan. Korean dislike of Japan and the arrogance Japan barely conceals in her relations with the Republic of Korea and in her attitude toward the more than 600,000 Koreans living in alien status in Japan are core realities in the Japan-Korea relationship that make accommodation difficult and rapprochement nearly impossible. The legacy of Japanese repression and brutality during thirty-five years of rule over Korea has left deep scars on Korean society and placed formidable obstacles in the way of a productive relationship.

Korean feelings about Japan were brought home in a compelling fashion during a conversation I recently had with a high-ranking Korean. In discussing Japanese-Korean relations, he said that Japan could never be trusted and would never be forgiven for the way Koreans were treated during the years Korea was a colony of Japan and for the way they are now being treated in Japan. His flushed face and clenched fists spoke eloquently of his passion. History provides persuasive evidence for this animosity. The struggle between China, Russia, and Japan for domination of the Korean peninsula was resolved decisively in Japan's favor as a consequence of the Russo-Japanese War of 1904–1905. Japanese annexation of Korea followed and lasted until 1945. During that time Korea was developed economically to serve the interests and meet the needs of Japan with only incidental concern for the Korean people. Korea was exploited economically and kept in political subjugation.

A Troubled History

Japan went so far as to adopt policies to separate the Korean people from their cultural identity. Efforts were made by Japanese administrators to substitute, where possible, Japanese for the Korean language. Korean literature and publications were suppressed and the Japanese, who comprised two percent of the population, were given preference over Koreans in the educational system. Japanese colonial rule offered few chances for Koreans to participate in government; the Japanese monopolized over 80 percent of top official positions, 60 percent of those at middle ranks, and 50 percent of the minor government jobs. Public land was expropriated and sold to Japanese on favorable terms, and the best privately owned property was force-sold to Japanese. Korean landowners who lost their property in this manner often migrated to Manchuria and beyond.

Policies followed by Japan provoked hostility and resistance, but

Korean protests were brutally crushed. Opposition to Japanese rule was stubborn, bitter, widespread and long-lasting. The independence movement finally had to go underground but continued to exert a strong influence on the Korean people. Japan's defeat in 1945 brought independence to Korea but only fleetingly. Korea was partitioned, had to endure a bloody civil war, and ever since has had to live with continuing tension, crisis, and threat. Thirteen years went by before Japan and the Republic of South Korea were able to agree on conditions for normalization of relations (Japan has never accorded diplomatic recognition to North Korea). Talks began in 1951 on finalizing a peace treaty, but it was not until 1964 that both sides made a concerted effort to accomplish normalization. Negotiations were difficult. Deep fears and apprehensions on the Korean side that Korea would once again be dominated by Japan, this time by economic not military force, inhibited progress. Opposition to the treaty in Korea was particularly strong and vocal, and it was only because of a determined stand by Korean President Park Chung-Hee that negotiations finally ended and a peace treaty was signed on June 22, 1965.

The ratification process evoked strong protests and demonstrations in Seoul and Tokyo and created constant turmoil in the parliaments of both countries. After a final stormy encounter with the opposition, the Korean government succeeded in ratifying the treaty in August 1965. It was then submitted to the Japanese Diet in October 1965, where it ran into a plethora of political barricades mounted by determined opposition parties, mostly in the form of disruptive maneuvers in the House of Representatives. The Japanese government was finally able to finesse the treaty through both houses of the Diet and by December 8, 1965, it had been ratified by both countries and was in effect.

Contemporary Problems

The treaty was an intricate document, reflecting the conflicting interests of the Republic of Korea and Japan over economic issues, territorial questions, fisheries, treatment of Koreans in Japan, and Japan's desire to have some flexibility in defining her relations with North Korea. The economic issue was ultimately reduced to a simple decision of how much aid Japan would give Korea. There were arguments over what to call the aid, Japan referring to it as "economic cooperation" and Korea calling it "claims" for hardships endured by Koreans under Japanese rule. In the end both sides described the aid in their own way. The fisheries problem was also difficult and complicated, made more so by the constant seizure of Japanese fishing boats that crossed the so-called "Rhee Line," delineating the areas allowed for fishing in Korean waters. A final complex settlement was reached, abolishing the Rhee Line, charting complicated fishing zones, and providing Japanese technical assistance to the Korean fishing industry.

With the solution of these touchy bilateral problems, ROK-Japanese relations from 1965 onward have generally centered on economic and trade questions, including Japanese support for South Korean industrial development. ROK-Japan trade has become a major issue in economic relations between the two countries. Primary causes are the large trade deficit that the ROK has incurred and growing competition in the world export market. As ROK exports have grown, it has needed more Japanese plants, equipment, and intermediate goods. Japan has sold Korea capital-intensive and advanced technological products, whereas South Korean exports to Japan have been either labor-intensive industrial goods or agricultural and fishery products. While the world economy was expanding along with South Korean exports, her trade deficit with Japan was manageable. However, when the world recession set in after 1979 and OPEC had to cancel many industrial projects in which the ROK was a prime contractor, South Korean income was reduced, competition with developing countries intensified, and her trade deficit with Japan became more burdensome.

Growing South Korean-Japanese competition for market shares in the United States, Europe, and Asia has aggravated overall trade relations and is having a special impact on the broad question of technology transfer, yet another area in Japanese-South Korean relations where economics, politics, and emotions become entangled. Contemporary Japanese-South Korean relations have also been clouded by non-economic problems, the more important and emotion-laden ones being the so-called textbook controversy, the Kim Dae-jung affair, and Japan's efforts to improve relations with North Korea.

The textbook issue began in 1982 and essentially involved the way Japan described her actions in China during World War II. In attempting to downplay the aggressive role of the Imperial Japanese Army in China and to minimize Japan's harsh rule in Korea, the Japanese Ministry of Education, in its textbook certification process, succeeded in antagonizing many in the educational profession in Japan and in provoking a storm of protest in China, North and South Korea, and in Southeast Asia. The Koreans were especially incensed when a Japanese cabinet member suggested that the Koreans had misrepresented Japan's administration of Korea in their own postwar textbooks. Japan's attempts to gloss over in this fashion her own guilt for actions in China and Korea and the stubborn refusal of LDP leaders to make any concessions to China and South Korea on the issue further inflamed relations.

The textbook controversy flared again in the summer of 1986. It differed from the earlier one in that the authors of the disputed textbook were a highly conservative group, the National Council to Protect Japan. Throughout the postwar era, authors of history texts tended to be liberal or left-wing scholars and professors engaged in an endless tug-of-war with the conservative Ministry of Education. Like the controversy in 1982, the later argument was between those in Japan who believed that the incident showed that Japan still had a long way to go to acknowledge past aggression and others who said that countries had no right to tell Japan how to teach its own history. The *Asahi Shimbun*, a major Japanese daily, in a biting editorial said that a more important issue was whether Japan remained insensitive to others' feelings. Why does Japan repeatedly offend its Asian neighbors? The very fact that the problem repeated itself, said the *Asahi*, makes one seriously suspect that all this expression of regret and contrition was more show than substance. Newspaper editorials in North and South Korea bitterly criticized Japan in June 1986 for what they called "this latest distortion of history" and warned that Japan must not forget what it did to Korea during the last war. The issue continues to smolder.

Another incident demonstrating the latent volatility in relations between Japan and South Korea was the so-called Kim Dae-jung affair. Kim, a leading Korean dissident, had run against President Park in 1971 and garnered over five million votes to Park's six million. After the election, Park declared martial law and the action was loudly denounced by Kim. On August 8, 1973, Kim was kidnapped from his Tokyo hotel room and taken to Seoul, Korea. The South Korean embassy in Tokyo was implicated. The Japanese government was deeply embarrassed, accused the ROK of violating Japanese sovereignty, and demanded that Kim be returned to Japan. The ROK refused. Negotiations began, and in November 1973, agreement was reached that Kim was to be free to leave Korea anytime he wished and that he would not be tried for any actions he had taken while in Japan (the reference was to inciting Japan to oppose President Park). In return, the Japanese government agreed to drop the issue.

The Kim Dae-jung incident fed the strong anti-Korean prejudices of many Japanese, strengthened the belief of intellectuals who opposed Japan's assertion of the correctness of their "progressive view" of the militarist South Korean regime, and allowed anti-Park forces in Japan and South Korea to coalesce around Kim in opposition to the Park regime. It was costly to President Park politically and economically, embarrassing to Japanese politicians in the ruling Liberal Democratic Party who were favorably disposed toward Park, and insulting to many Japanese who believed their sovereignty had been trampled on by the Koreans.

More fundamental to Japan-Korea relations, however, is the sensitive security issue. Korea has always been linked to Japan's security. When President-elect Jimmy Carter announced in late 1976 that he intended to begin withdrawing U.S. military forces from South Korea after his inauguration, Japanese leaders were filled with dread. Traditionally, Japan has looked on Korea as a dagger pointed at her heart. Korea in the hands of a hostile power was always regarded as a military threat. The Japanese were concerned that Mr. Carter's decision might persuade the North Koreans to try again to conquer the South. Under such circumstances, they wondered if they could continue to have faith in the United States as a dependable ally. Mr. Carter wisely withdrew his proposal in the face of strong opposition in the U.S. Senate and from America's allies.

The Japanese would have to face internal political conflict, problems in relations with Russia and China, and the use of American bases in Japan to support the ROK and U.S. military forces in Korea, should fighting break out on the Korean peninsula. Japan's efforts to improve relations with North Korea have also been watched with a wary eye by the ROK. The main Japanese impetus has been economic—to increase trade with North Korea. Given the heavily centralized nature of the North Korean economy, the Japanese have had only limited success. Japan's relations with North Korea are likely to be limited for the foreseeable future. If Japan's goal is to further the process of reconciliation between the two Koreas, she must be careful not to move too boldly to disturb the process. And she must recognize that the citizens of North Korea harbor the same emotions about Japan as do the people in South Korea.

The Japanese government is therefore strongly motivated to contribute to peace in Korea. Her efforts to encourage the ROK, to maintain good relations with North Korea, and to direct her energies toward promoting reconciliation between North and South Korea are all evidence of her desire to see peace and stability on the peninsula. Japan will probably continue to support the presence of American troops in South Korea as a deterrent to any North Korean military move south. Although Japan has no security relationship with the ROK, her political and logistical support for the U.S. security commitment to the ROK is a vital element in maintaining peace in the area.

C
H
A
P
T
E
R
10

WILL JAPAN FACE HER INTERNATIONAL RESPONSIBILITIES?

Japan faces the challenges of the next century still dominated by values that reach back into the deep recesses of her history, by an insular outlook that has been shaped by her geographic position, and by the stark reality of a changing world that is pressing her to assert responsible leadership commensurate with her economic power.

Can Japan meet the challenge? Can the Japanese people accommodate to the new forces that are reshaping the world order? To judge the prospects, it may be helpful to look again at the behavioral patterns of the Japanese and their capacity to reorder their society, and to emphasize their difference from American values and deportment.

A typical Japanese, as David MacEachron of the Japan Society has noted, is different from the typical American—if there is such a thing—in several important respects. To a much greater extent than his American counterpart, the Japanese is aware that he or she is part of an important continuum—family, village, firm, nation—which is essentially immortal, and which the individual must help to maintain during his relatively brief life. The unbridled individualism exalted in America, by contrast, must in the end lead to defeat and despair, if the individual sees his or her mortal self as the highest good. The Japanese are willing, by and large, to commit themselves much more intensely to whatever they fix on—whether craft, employment, friends or family—than is common in the United States. There are, of course, many in the United States who give themselves unstintingly to a profession or a human institution, but the extent to which this prevails in Japan is remarkable.

The Japanese, more than their American counterparts, practice the goal of self-education. They are prodigious consumers of books and magazines. A considerable portion of the population are amateur musicians, and all sorts of visual arts from calligraphy to painting are widely practiced. Over a lifetime, they believe, there is without question more enjoyment to be derived from the pleasures of the mind than from the pleasures of the flesh. The Japanese by no means neglect the latter, and, unlike many in the United States who still suffer from a Puritan heritage, they have no guilt about enjoying them. The unabashed Japanese attention to the joys of the mind, however, contributes to their sense of well-being.

There is nothing in the American life-style to prevent us from deepening our own enjoyment of life by learning more about the incredible natural and man-created wonders that surround us in the world we are allowed to visit so briefly. We can study the ways of others who have learned the art of living and perhaps thereby increase our own joy in living. If Americans look at Japanese, they will discover that self-discipline, commitment to some worthy endeavor, willingness to work hard at one's job—not simply to earn a living but because it is socially useful—and a greater concentration on the beauties of nature and of man contribute significantly to the feeling that life is worth living.

Today, much emphasis is being placed in Japan on the need to internationalize. The term internationalization as applied to Japan is an oft-used code word that means different things to different people. It is now popular terminology in Japan, where it connotes a new frontier toward which the Japanese believe they must travel if they are to satisfy their longing for recognition as a major world power. For most Japanese, however, the drive for international recognition is painful. Japan, as we have seen, has a legacy of geographic and political isolation and this has bred an insularity in the Japanese psyche that makes them suspicious of foreigners or "outsiders." The word *gaijin*, or foreign person, is used liberally by Japanese and carries a certain innuendo that is palpable to foreigners who live and work in Japan. Will these attributes prepare Japanese to accept their international responsibilities; to confront an international society that they read about but have no particular desire to emulate?

A Japan committed to a more prominent international role will have important consequences for U.S.-Japan relations. As Japan takes on more international responsibilities and her confidence grows, she will begin to exert greater independence from the United States in foreign affairs. While evidence of such independence is meager at the moment, growing nationalism and a sense of pride in being one of the world's economic giants will propel Japan onto the international stage, but at a slow, careful, and measured pace. Given the configuration of international power politics and Japan's continued reticence to assert herself diplomatically in the face of superpower confrontation, all evidence points to the United States remaining the cornerstone of Japanese foreign policy and security.

Japan's spectacular success in international trade and commerce has done nothing to diminish either her belief in her own uniqueness or the conviction of other nations that Japan is inbred and culturally alienated from the rest of the world. A sense of isolation has pervaded Japanese consciousness throughout the whole of the modern era. The Japanese are very private people in their personal lives, not given easily to personal commitments and the costs which they may exact. Moreover, Japanese political culture does not lend itself easily to international relations among equals. The very facts of Japanese development have set the nation apart. Japan is of the West but of the East as well. This national schizophrenia over her international identity influences Japan's relations with other states and is a hindrance to efforts to advance more forcefully onto the international stage.

Japanese leaders often speak of the limitations on Japan's ability to move in the direction of a new internationalism; whereas they formerly played on the theme of "Japan is poor" to explain their reluctance to assume international responsibilities, they now use the thesis that "Japan is vulnerable."

Japan remains a nation obsessed with its own future. The postwar dynamics of her economy have triggered a latent propensity for self-analysis. The Japanese endlessly analyze and anticipate the twists and turns that lie ahead. Government agencies churn out reports projecting the future course of the economy, suggesting what steps Japan should take to adapt. Polls charting what people think may happen in the next decade or two abound.

Government officials worry about the rapid aging of the Japanese population and the resulting strains on public pensions, health care, and insurance costs. Doubts are also expressed whether the younger generation is ready and willing to embrace the ethic of hard work and self-sacrifice that underpins the nation's success. There is a widespread conviction that children who have grown up in affluence cannot be as driven as were their parents, whose memories of poverty fueled their dedication. Complaints about the attitude of young Japanese are legion. It is commonplace, for example, to hear older Japanese tell of company trainees who leave work early. Yet many Japanese still hope that traditional attitudes will prevail.

The Japanese are not a people who like surprises, but they have been schooled by their own history to expect sudden turns of fortune. To worry about problems in advance is one way of planning how to ovecome them. This preoccupation with self, while nurturing a determination to succeed as a society and produce a more satisfactory way of life, has been a handicap to those Japanese who believe that the time has come for Japan to assume greater international responsibility. These advocates are the so-called reformers. They call for greater openness to the outside world. They insist that Japan must accept foreigners in its society, even if Japanese homogeneity is threatened; that Japan must learn how to accept diversity, for without such adjustments, both in attitudes and economic structure, much of Japan's assiduous planning for the future could be in vain.

The Japanese people find it hard to think of Japan as a major economic power when they still have to work so hard and endure what is, by the standards of other industrialized nations, substandard housing. There is a major disparity between the image Japan projects to the outside world and the feelings Japanese have about themselves. This discrepancy is the source of much misunderstanding and confusion.

These sociocultural conditions and geopolitical factors continue to obstruct Japan's acceptance of international responsibility. One might ask, is the concept of internationalism a mere vogue that fashionable Japanese bureaucrats appear to be promoting, and is the price of assuming Japan's place in world politics as the second largest producing nation a burden that its citizens are willing to bear? Skeptical Japanese analysts would reply that many Japanese citizens seem eager to accept the rewards of an internationalized Japan, including enhanced national prestige, but few are ready to make the necessary sacrifices. True internationalism requires self-initiative in defining one's own proper role in the world without having to be forced to accept it.

Japanese society is so rigidly structured, so hierarchical in positioning its citizens in relationship to one another, so concerned about the impact of foreign influences on its homogeneity, so reluctant to accept back into the fold those sturdy, ambitious, and inquiring Japanese who spend time in foreign countries learning new languages and new cultures, that a reordering of national priorities is imperative before Japan can finally become a full participant on the international stage.

Reluctance to change, for example, can be seen in the way society treats Japanese citizens, mostly young people, who have spent time in foreign countries. Upon their return to Japan they are greeted by some harsh realities. Their slight deficiencies (not having memorized the same numbers of *kanji* as their stay-at-home cousins) are emphasized, they are treated as not quite fully Japanese, and many are tainted to the point that they can band together only with other so-called "returnees." These culturally disenfranchised Japanese must be "deinternationalized" if they hope to be assimilated into the mainstream of society. This situation suggests to some inside and outside Japan that Japanese who are both fully Japanese and also truly international-minded (*kokusai teki*) only cultivate such an image in front of foreigners, while reverting to a mere superficial form of international-mindedness when among fellow Japanese. Those Japanese who worry about such things are looking for signs of change, for evidence that Japan is at last beginning to shake off her introvertedness.

I f she succeeds, it will be due in large measure to the reformers referred to earlier, the new business and political leaders who recognize that the reality for Japan is to assume the full responsibilities of international citizenship. Prime Minister Nakasone is the leader in efforts to move Japan toward greater international responsibility. He says that this means much more than buying foreign goods, traveling abroad, and making an appearance at summit meetings. People tend to focus on economics because Japan is an economic country, but there are also deep cultural and moral undertones in the debate, a fear of losing old values without establishing new ones. The more profound aspects of the debate are being ignored by most Japanese, replaced by talk of the damage the fast-rising yen is doing to jobs and businesses that depend on exports. The mood is aggrieved. There is little discussion about benefits from a strong yen, the cheaper imports, lower consumer prices, more non-inflationary growth.

While Japan is a collectivist society based on capitalism, the reformers' underlying notion is that Japan needs to spur individual creativity, individual enterprise, even at the cost of breaking the conformist mold and accepting more diversity. For now, however, there are no guidelines, no models for Japan to follow. As one veteran Japan observer noted, when riches become a burden they should be given away. But the Christian tradition of charity is not a part of the Confucian order. Japan must learn about giving, he said, as well as earning.

Japan is beginning to learn about ways of providing financial and economic assistance to less developed countries as a means of asserting her internationalism. The prime motivator is Mr. Nakasone, who combines the charisma of a Kennedy with the zest of a Reagan. Over the past year, he has battled his own bureaucrats to open Japan's markets; managed negotiations to try to satisfy angry congressmen in Washington; appeared on television urging his countrymen to buy foreign products and reduce Japan's trade surplus; defended the 40 percent rise in the value of the yen vis-a-vis the dollar, which is so painful to Japanese exporters; recently staged a successful summit conference in Tokyo; and maneuvered his powerful party rivals into an election at a time they didn't want one and, in electioneering, was ebullient, acting out the role of an American politician. On July 6, 1986, his party won a stunning victory.

Young voters appreciate his aggressive self-confidence, his ability to rub shoulders as an equal with President Reagan, Prime Minister Margaret Thatcher, and President Francois Mitterrand. Mr. Nakasone believes that Japanese must re-enter the world as a confident people if they are to accept international burdens. To do so they must continue to rely on their old values and traditions. He has been a strong advocate of economic, educational, and administrative reform, and has given leadership to a number of policies intended to advance the cause of internationalism in Japan.

On the economic and foreign assistance side, the Ministry of International Trade and Industry (MITI) published a study on April 18, 1986 urging a global role for Japan. The report contained a seven-point proposal to achieve this goal, including the liberalization of trade and greater direct investment. It stressed that the world is facing radical changes triggered mainly by advances in information-related technology; that the international community is on the threshold of a new industrial revolution and that the global economic structure as well as political and social systems will be affected. It underlined the need for Japan to reconsider its role in the global community by taking a more positive approach to its international responsibilities. Japan must reject pacifism in international affairs, make a more substantial contribution to the economic and cultural well-being of others, and strive to improve Asia's stability and economic development. Experts believe the report will have an important impact on Japan's future policy planning. It was compiled by twenty-five authorities, including nine foreigners, in such fields as political science, technology, economics, and culture.

Japan is also stepping up its Overseas Development Aid (ODA). The ODA program is popular in Japan, not only with the progressives, who feel that Japan has left a legacy of colonialism, particularly in Asia, that still hurts Japan's image in those regions and that ODA is a way of rectifying that wrong, but also among conservatives who see ODA as a way for Japan to exercise reasonable leadership and play a more important role in the world. The years 1984 and 1985 were milestones in the expansion of Japan's international economic assistance programs, in terms of the scale of assistance and of a renewed commitment to helping less developed countries.

With ODA amounting to $4.32 billion in 1984, Japan overtook France to become the second largest contributor—following the United States—among the seventeen industrialized members of the Development Assistance Committee of the Organization of Economic Cooperation and Development. In a speech before the United Nations in October 1985, Prime Minister Nakasone pledged to double ODA by the end of 1992, and declared that it is the moral duty and major international responsibility of Japan to use its economic strength and technological expertise to assist developing nations.

Former Japanese Foreign Minister Okita Saburo also expressed Japan's determination to play a more significant role in international affairs. Speaking before a gathering of scientists and economists at the first Global Infrastructure Projects Conference held in Anchorage, Alaska on July 11, 1986, he declared that Japan is moving toward the creation of a global "Marshall Plan" to provide significant funds for technological projects, and proclaimed that the Japanese government would take the first step to contribute one-tenth of one percent of her GNP to set up an international fund, while simultaneously inviting other industrial countries to do the same. Okita emphasized that the time had come for Japan to take the initiative in global affairs. Delegates to the conference were said to be stunned by the Japanese proposal, one observing that "most of us feel that we were present at a historic event."

Japan has taken other actions recently to demonstrate her intention to play a more active international role. She sent invitations to the governments of Britain, Canada, France, West Germany, Italy, and the United States to join a new international effort to explore the frontiers of science. The Japanese government said it was prepared to pledge $5 billion over the next decade to finance the proposed research program, which it called "Human Frontiers."

Some experts see the Japanese plan as a civilian equivalent to President Reagan's SDI program. Funds to carry out the research would be provided by MITI and allocated to universities and research institutes in the six participating countries. European skeptics generally familiar with the Japanese proposal believe it is essentially intended to improve Japan's political image in the West by showing that Japan is spending some of its huge trade surplus on a project of benefit to Western nations. The program would also place heavy emphasis on problems of particular interest to Japan itself, such as urban overcrowding, pollution, and the difficulties of an aging population. These are the issues Japan must solve if she is to forge ahead.

In another effort to take a leadership role, Foreign Minister Abe and top Japanese business leaders met in late January 1986 to explore ways of encouraging economic growth in ASEAN countries. Japan absorbs only 10 percent of ASEAN's total exports compared to 30 percent for the United States. Japan also accounts for 15 percent of the total output of goods produced in Japanese-financed factories in ASEAN countries. Abe emphasized to the dozen industrialists present from the Federation of Economic Organizations, the Japanese Chamber of Commerce and Industry, and Japan's Committee for Economic Development that Japan must do more to support economic, political, and cultural relations with ASEAN nations.

In still another endeavor, the powerful Japanese business organization, the Committee for Economic Development (*Keizai Doyukai*), in a white paper for business enterprises issued on January 27, 1986, called on Japanese companies to prepare for the internationalization of business activities. The paper noted that more Japanese firms will undertake production, financial management, research and development, and other activities in foreign countries, and stressed the importance of nurturing the "international businessman" who, with knowledge of the history, culture, and customs of the countries involved, would be capable of managing a successful business abroad.

Under Mr. Nakasone, steps have also been taken to reform the educational system and "internationalize" the legal profession. The prime minister established an educational reform committee in 1985 to explore ways of changing some of the basic assumptions underlying the educational organization in Japan. Under his prodding, the Japan Federation of Bar Associations in December 1985 also approved a government proposal to conditionally allow qualified foreign lawyers to practice in Japan.

Much of what Japan is doing today to move more purposefully onto the international stage had its genesis in the late 1970s when then Prime Minister Ohira Masayoshi fathered the doctrine of comprehensive security. This concept argued that Japan's security involved political, military, and economic efforts and that all three should be seen within a common framework. The comprehensive security principle suggests that Japan has interests at stake in the world and must be committed to support the strategic interests she has in common with her Western allies. By adopting the notion of comprehensive security, Ohira was arguing that economic aid is a valid way of advancing these security interests.

In adding up the moves taken so far by Japan to become more internationalist, the question is often asked, will Japan persevere, and what are some of the problems that confront this dynamic society as it moves tentatively into the twenty-first century? Among others, are these three major issues:

- Forty years after a calamitous wartime defeat, followed by a stunning peacetime rebirth, Japan has evolved into an ambivalent world power. It is proud of its economic achievements, but it also knows that this success has made others edgy or outright angry.

- Japan is obsessed with the notion that it is a unique nation. Yet, self-consciously, it measures virtually every accomplishment against those of other countries, from the size of its GNP to the prowess of its home-run hitters.

- The Japanese boast in more expansive moments that the next century will belong to them. Then, in the next breath, they retreat to the safety of the tattered cliché that theirs is a "resource-poor island country" hardly destined for such a grand role. Japan has, in fact, become a very rich country but up to now has generally shied away from the global obligations that come with being rich.

The debate has gone on for several years and Japan is slowly changing. It has become more outspoken, more eager to offer other countries economic aid, more willing to talk about an increased defense effort. Prime Minister Nakasone promises more to come. But most of these tentative steps have been carefully measured, and even the smallest ones produce a national angst. Japan remains a reactive power, responding to outside pressures for economic liberalization of its markets and to demands that she assume more international responsibilities.

Thus far the Japanese, as we noted earlier, have not figured out how to become a global force without scaring themselves and everyone else. Mr. Nakasone and like-minded nationalists talk a good deal about traditional values and a renewal of the Japanese spirit. Some foreigners, hearing these things, wonder whether Japan is moving back toward prewar days when the emperor was venerated and *bushido*, the spirit of the warrior, was in vogue. ASEAN nations worry about all this and so do many Japanese. Some Japanese retain a broad pacifist streak. Others are hardly pacifist, but somewhat gun-shy.

They do not want to repeat the adventures that led them into World War II and total defeat.

There is also the cynical, cost-effective approach: Why do more for the world than necessary? Japan has managed to get by with the best possible defense policy, one in which someone else pays for it, namely the United States, a nation that also worries about Japan's foreign policy.

Overseas critics have grown weary of these ambivalent attitudes. To most of them, Japan is untrustworthy. The country accumulates more and more money but does little to help maintain the world order from which it prospers. Edwin Reischauer, former U.S. Ambassador to Japan, recently said that there is something unhealthy about a country as economically powerful and technologically advanced as Japan attempting to remain politically out of sight. This falsifies the real situation, creating confusion and suspicion among others and breeding resentment within Japan itself. But many Japanese, especially older ones, seem genuine in regarding Japan as weak and politically impotent. They do not understand why foreigners feel differently. Japan has not learned to think like a rich man, a leading politician said recently. At times this poor-man view assumes a chip-on-the-shoulder edge, sharpened by a conviction that other nations view Japan as a parvenu, clever but basically imitative. Japanese are painfully aware that they are the only non-Western member of the "big power club."

Japan remains, therefore, what it has always been, a country that considers itself an outsider in a confusing, sometimes unfriendly world. Changes in the Japanese people's psychology take a long time, said Mr. Amaya Naohiro, president of the Japan Economic Foundation, noting that for 2000 years Japan has lived outside the international community. Even now people do not feel that Japan is the center of the world. They still believe that Japan is a small fish in the great Pacific Ocean; yet the Pacific can be a comforting, nurturing ocean, keeping trouble safely away. Japanese are knowledgeable about the United States and other countries, but the world does not often break through its insularity.

The most serious question is whether the Japanese can see themselves as the world sees them, drop their insularity, and recognize that success creates responsibilities. From what I have observed in talking with Japanese politicians, businessmen, journalists, students, barbers, professors, shoe salesmen, housewives, and diplomats, among others, there is a slow but steady trend toward accepting the reality of Japan's participation in international affairs. The bearings Japan has established for her advance onto the international stage have not been determined without substantial prodding from the outside world.

Certainly trade has been a primary stimulus. As Japan continues to expand her economic reach, she seems to be making a greater effort to understand her neighbors, to give aid to less developed countries, to take initiatives in the political sphere (most notably her support for the Western response to the Rangoon bombings, the KAL shootdown, the invasions of Afghanistan and Cambodia, and the sanctions against Poland), to overcome personal feelings of insecurity, to appreciate that her success usually creates jealousies and animosities, and to cope with the realities of her prominent position in the family of nations. Japan has been an international shut-in for many years. She will not be able to continue a wide expansion of her economic interests in East Asia without taking on greater political responsibilities there. Japan is also aware of the uneasiness about her intentions in China, Korea, and Southeast Asia and consequently practices a low posture in foreign affairs. It is difficult to get a consensus in Japan on any foreign policy that might present either responsibilities or risks. The men who have risen to leadership in postwar Japan have been responsive to this public mood.

But Japan is coming under increasing pressure to abandon its detachment. As the Chinese saying goes, they have been privileged to "sit on the mountain and watch the tigers fight." Now they must grapple more and more with tough problems directly involving national interests. The internationalization of Japan has begun and, from all available evidence, a consensus is growing in Japanese society that it is a burden that must be borne, however challenging to built-in beliefs and painful to age-old values and cultural traditions. The steps will be hesitant, the desire still strong to avoid conflict and controversy. But her power and economic strength leave her no choice but to accept the challenge of her impatient allies and to participate along with them in establishing some kind of stability in the world order.

The most impatient of Japan's allies is the United States, which is anxious for Japan to assume more of the burden for her own security, work more closely in developing financial and economic policies to stabilize the international economic order, share more of her resources to assist less developed countries to build their economies, and take a more positive role in settling the world's political, economic, and security problems.

A more aggressive and active Japan would very likely be a less compliant partner in the U.S.-Japan relationship. But it is important to remember that the two countries share common interests and values that continue to provide strong underpinnings to their relationship.

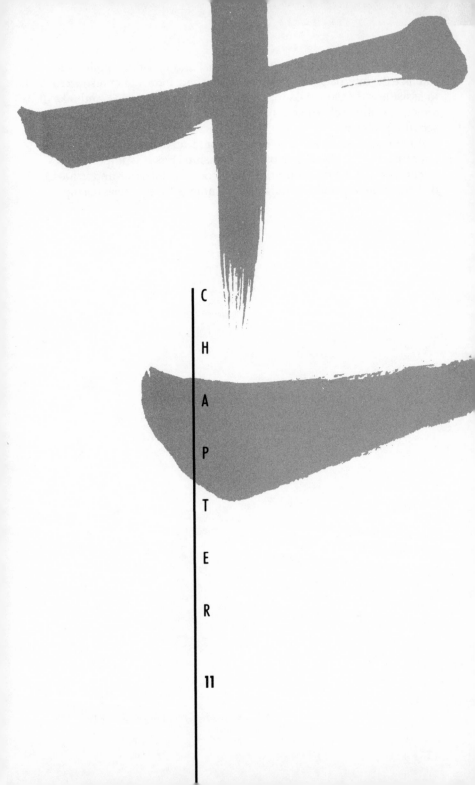

C
H
A
P
T
E
R

11

Relations between the United States and Japan have been marked by harmony as well as rivalry since Commodore Perry's "black ships" opened Japan to the world in 1853. The competitive spirit has left its imprint. From Perry to Reagan, the two countries have known periods of calm and friction, war and the threat of war, intense economic rivalry, immigration tensions, and above all, an uncertainty bred of ignorance and lack of mutual understanding.

The roller coaster relationship started with Perry threatening the Tokugawa Shogunate with naval bombardment if it refused to open Japan to world commerce and has come full circle with officials of the Reagan administration and members of Congress threatening Japan with protectionist legislation because of the "closed Japanese market." It is the story of two intensely energetic and patriotic peoples, one homogeneous, the other heterogeneous, both occupying highly strategic geographic positions and so diverse in culture, mores, and language that communication has been difficult at best.

Because of its importance to the entire world, the urgent need for better understanding between these two nations cannot be overlooked, but there is uncertainty

THE FUTURE: RIVALRY OR HARMONY?

about how to proceed, and more trials and frustrations and more economic, political, and security conflicts lie ahead.

Despite the current catalog of troubles, however, the alliance has important strengths: The two economies are moving from alignment to integration; American markets remain open to Japanese goods; jobs for American workers in Japanese factories located in the United States are increasing; Japanese purchase of U.S. Treasury bonds is growing; energetic and restless American corporations are having more success in penetrating the Japanese market; and cooperation in space, energy conservation, environmental protection, and medical research is expanding. All these things are evidence of a thriving relationship that has brought peace, stability, and economic opportunity to the Pacific Basin.

During the years I lived in Japan, I observed many of the developments in the relationship that John Emmerson and I have borne witness to in this book. I have talked with frustrated American businessmen who misunderstood their Japanese counterparts and left Japan embittered and mistrustful. I have noted the long, weary hours put in by Christian missionaries in their attempts to bring the gospel to a people who are comfortable with their Confucian, Buddhist, and Shinto teachings. (Despite the efforts of these disciples of the church, the number of Japanese Christians has never exceeded one percent of the population). I have listened with admiration and awe to the stories of human suffering and deprivation endured as Japan pulled itself up from what must have been the nadir of its history—total defeat and devastation in World War II. I have seen how these remarkable people, through dedication, hard work, perseverance, self-discipline, and a deep belief in the worth of their country and its traditions, have created an economic miracle that has astonished much of mankind but, unfortunately, has also aroused jealousy, envy, mistrust, and hatred in many parts of the world. The Japanese are aware of this but are uncertain about how to deal with it. What is most troublesome for them is their sense of the growing enmity in the United States triggered by their success.

The acrimony and hot words between Tokyo and Washington are seeping into the marrow of the relationship and beginning to poison the atmosphere. I deeply regret the retrogression that is taking place in the relationship, but I think it is temporary. There will continue to be economic rivalry as there has been in the past, but I also foresee a further incorporation of the two economic systems that will bring both countries into a closer and more productive relationship. Harmony, or *wa* in Japanese, may not be a prominent staple of the alliance, but it will still exert a positive influence because it is so basic to Japanese *kangaekata,* or "the thinking way."

The desire of the Japanese to learn English so they can relate more effectively to Americans and to other English-speaking peoples is particularly encouraging. I regret that my own countrymen do not share a similar enthusiasm for learning Japanese. The ambition of Japanese to reach out beyond their shores to communicate more efficiently with other countries is heartening to those who believe Japan has a much more important role to play in world affairs than she has undertaken in the past.

I feel less sanguine about the American response. The United States, with commitments that gird the globe, is preoccupied with its leadership role and seems uncertain about how to make a positive response to the Japanese economic challenge, beyond grumbling about Japanese unfairness and passing protective legislation to deal with that "unfairness." It is not a healthy reaction—yet, I suppose, a predictable one, given the frustrations caused by our loss of world economic dominance in the last several decades and the heavy responsibilities of free-world leadership.

As the two countries approach the twenty-first century, the economic, political, and security links being forged today will provide a strong basis for survivability of the alliance, even though the two countries will continue to experience intense economic competition and misunderstandings over defense issues.

What, in the end, does all this tell us about the U.S.-Japan relationship?

First of all, it tells us that the United States and Japan have become strongly interdependent. A healthy economy in one country is a prerequisite for a vigorous economy in the other. This has been true for the past thirty-five years and, barring an international economic upheaval, will continue to hold true.

Secondly, it demonstrates that even though we have come to depend on each other, our interests diverge. But the fact that the U.S.-Japan relationship is critical to continued peace and prosperity in Northeast Asia cannot be overlooked, and where differences exist, they must be negotiated and bargains struck.

The U.S.-Japan alliance, as Prime Minister Nakasone Yasuhiro likes to refer to it, has survived many crises since the first security treaty in 1951. There have been anti-base and anti-nuclear demonstrations against the United States (President Eisenhower's trip to Japan in 1960 had to be cancelled because of such demonstrations); there was turmoil over the reversion of Okinawa, bitterness caused by the so-called "Nixon shocks" and the sudden shift in America's China policy, and continuing tension and friction over deepening trade problems. Despite it all, both sides have coped well because it is in their common interests to do so.

Just before his death in March 1984, John Emmerson made the following astute observation about U.S.-Japan relations: "Until Prime Minister Nakasone used the word 'alliance' to describe the relationship between Japan and the United States, this designation had not been fully accepted. When the word first appeared in a joint communique at the time of Prime Minister Suzuki Zenko's visit to the United States in May 1981, a storm of protest arose in Tokyo. During the 1960s and 1970s, the word 'partnership' was deliberately used to avoid a military connotation to the relations between the two countries. One can therefore say that at last the two Pacific neighbors have duly and formally recognized the alliance which binds them together. Thus a kind of turning point can be said to have been reached."

SUGGESTED READING ▌

Hugh Borton. *Japan's Modern Century: From Perry to 1970*. New York: Ronald Press, 1970.

Chong-Sik Lee. *Japan and Korea*. Stanford, Calif.: Hoover Institution Press, 1985.

Ralph Clough. *East Asia and U.S. Security*. Washington, D.C.: Brookings, 1974.

John K. Emmerson. *Arms, Yen, and Power: The Japanese Dilemma*. New York: Dunellen, 1971.

————. *The Japanese Thread*. New York: Holt, Rinehart and Winston, 1978.

A. Whitney Griswold. *The Far East Policy of the United States*. New Haven, Conn.: Yale University Press, 1968.

Townsend Harris. *The Complete Journal of Townsend Harris, First American Consul General and Minister to Japan*. New York: Doubleday and Co., 1930.

Harrison M. Holland. *Managing Diplomacy: The United States and Japan*. Stanford, Calif.: Hoover Institution Press, 1984.

George B. Sansom. *Japan: A Short Cultural History*. London: The Cresset Press, 1932.

Robert Scalapino. *Asia and the Road Ahead*. Berkeley, Calif.: University of California Press, 1975.

Harold Vinacke. *A History of the Far East in Modern Times*. New York: Appleton-Century-Crofts, 1950.

John K. Emmerson

Harrison M. Holland

ABOUT THE AUTHORS

John K. Emmerson, in the words of former U.S. Ambassador to Japan and noted Harvard scholar Edwin O. Reischauer, was "perhaps the leading Japanese expert of his generation in the American Foreign Service."

Mr. Emmerson entered the Foreign Service in 1935 and was assigned various posts in Osaka, Tapei, Taiwan, and Tokyo. He returned to Washington to serve in the Division of Far Eastern Affairs of the Department of State, and from 1943 to 1945 was political adviser to General Joseph Stilwell in the China-Burma-India Theatre. He later served as political adviser to the Commander-in-Chief of the U.S. Pacific Fleet and to General MacArthur in Japan.

From 1952 to 1962, Mr. Emmerson filled diplomatic posts in a great variety of countries—Pakistan, Lebanon, France, Nigeria, and the Federation of Rhodesia and Nyasaland, returning in 1962 to Tokyo as minister and deputy chief of mission.

In January 1967 Mr. Emmerson came to Stanford as diplomat-in-residence and senior research fellow at the Hoover Institution, continuing as a consultant to the U.S. Department of State and the Institute for Defense Analysis. A prolific writer, his latest book was *The Japanese Thread: A Life in the U.S. Foreign Service*, published in 1978 by Holt, Rinehart, and Winston.

Mr. Emmerson died in 1984, and was posthumously awarded the

Second Class Order of the Sacred Treasure by the Japanese government. His reputation as a distinguished scholar and diplomat will long survive.

Harrison Holland's fascination with the Orient began in his college days at the University of Washington, where in 1944 he earned his B.A. in East Asian Studies. From 1947 to 1954 he served as an international relations officer at the U.S. Department of State, and from 1954 to 1971 as a U.S. Foreign Service officer in Japan, meanwhile earning his Ph.D. in Japanese political studies from George Washington University.

In Japan, Professor Holland mastered Japanese, negotiated the U.S.-Japan Consular Convention in 1960–1962, and from 1962 to 1966 was the U.S. Embassy officer responsible for all matters concerning the U.S.-Japan Security Treaty.

Since 1971, Professor Holland has brought his experience to the academic world, first as diplomat-in-residence and then as Professor of Japanese Studies at San Francisco State University, where in 1973 he founded the U.S.-Japan Institute and served as its director until 1980. He has been visiting professor at Keio University in Tokyo and visiting scholar at the Hoover Institution at Stanford. Since 1981 he has been a research scholar at the Northeast Asia–United States Forum on International Policy at Stanford.

A prolific writer, Harrison Holland has published books on Japanese history and diplomacy and written numerous articles. His most recent book, *Managing Defense: Japan's Dilemma*, is a 1987 joint publication of the University Press of America and the Woodrow Wilson Center. Mr. Holland continues to nurture his contacts with Japanese friends and colleagues, so that he brings to his work an understanding not only of the Japanese economy and government but also a deep familiarity with the Japanese people.

INDEX ■

78–79; safety of, 79; scoffed at, 49; in U.S. market, 9, 76–80

Automobiles, U.S.: in Japanese market, 80, 81, 117; production of, 76, 77, 78

Automotive plants, Japanese: productivity in, 78–79; in U.S., 109, 115

Automotive plants, U.S.: closing of, 77, 78; Japanese cars produced in, 77–78, 80

Aviation agreement: Soviet-Japanese, 145

Axis: Japan's adherence to, 52

Baker, James, 99

Bakufu ("tent government"), 35

Bankers Trust, 103

Bank of Japan, 85, 89, 101

Banks, Japanese: discount rate cut by, 101–102

Bashi Channel, 138

Beef production: and Japanese protectionism, 69, 70

Biddle, James, 41

"Bill of Rights": Meiji, 38; postwar Japanese, 58

Bonds: and access to Japan's capital market, 104; U.S. Treasury, Japanese investment in, 104, 108, 178

Braselton, Georgia, 109

Brooke, Lieutenant, 45

Buchanan, James, 45

Buddhism/Buddhists, 6, 22, 29–30, 32, 33, 34, 178; Shingon sect of, 32; Zen, 33

Budget deficit: Japanese, 68, 126; U.S., 7, 11, 117, 126

Buick, 81

Burakumin ("invisible race"), 26

Bureaucratic infighting, Japanese, 126

Bushido (code of warrior), 14, 25, 154

Business activities, Japanese: internationalization of, 171

California, 42; alien land laws of, 47; Japanese companies in, 107, 115; Japanese food imports from, 10

Cambodia, 151; Vietnamese invasion of, 14, 174

Canada, 170

Capek, Karel, 75

Capital markets, Japanese: need for U.S. access to, 90, 98, 103–105

Capitol Beltway, Washington, D.C., 74

Carter, Jimmy, 155, 160

Chang An, 33

Charity: Japanese and, 168

Charter Oath, Meiji, 38

Chase Manhattan, 103

Chiang Kai-shek, 62, 148, 149

Children, Japanese: lack of traditional attitudes among, 166

China: aggressiveness of Japan in, 158–59; and conflict over Korea, 156; defeated by Japan, 46, 128; early influence on Japan, 29–33; Hideyoshi's plan to conquer, 35, 39; Nationalists vs. Japanese in, 50, 52, 129, 142, 148; U.S.-Japan conflict over, 48–49, 50–52, 55, 57; U.S. "Open Door" policy for, 47, 50; Western dismemberment of, 27. *See also* People's Republic of China; Sino-Japanese relations; Sino-Japanese War; Taiwan

"China boom," 152

"China incident," 66

China Sea, 42, 141

"China shock," 62

Chinese Communist Party: Japanese party's break with, 59

Chinese ideographs: in Japanese language, 20, 30, 32

Chinese Nationalists: vs. Japanese, 50, 52, 129, 142, 148; in Taiwan, 148, 149

Chinese people: in Japan, 21, 26; tensions between Japanese and, 140, 153–154

Choshu, 37

Chou En-lai, 151

Christians in Japan: crucified, 34; percentage of, 178. *See also* Missionaries

Chronicles of Japan (*Nihongi*), 20

Chrysler: bail-out of, 84; and productivity, 79

Churchill, Winston, 54, 66

Civics (Honda), 109

Class distinctions, Japanese, 26, 36; discarded, 38. *See also* Hierarchies

Climate of Japan, 23

Coal industry, Japanese, 83

Columbus (U.S. warship), 41

Committee for Economic Development, Japanese, 171

"Committee of One Hundred Seeking a Revision of the Japan-U.S. Security Treaty," 123–124

Communication: U.S.-Japan cooperation in improving, 7

Communism: Japan as U.S. ally against, 60, 120; as world threat, 119–120

Communist China. *See* People's Republic of China

Communists, Japanese, 9; ebbing strength of, 59

Community, Japanese sense of, 25

Companies, Japanese: profits of, 68; rivalry among, 70–71; and robotics, 75; in U.S. and overseas (*see* Investments, Japanese)

Companies, U.S.: in Japan, 151

Competition: in automobile market, 77; declining in U.S. industry, 8; for Japanese investments, 11, 115–116; for market shares, 158; U.S.-Japan, 6 (*see also* U.S.-Japan trade: tensions over)

Comprehensive security, doctrine of, 171

Computers, 74; imbalance of U.S.-Japan trade in, 69, 91, 94

Confucianism, 22, 25, 29, 30, 32, 168, 178

Constitution, Japanese: Article 9, and disarmament, 8, 12, 13, 59, 71, 120, 121–122, 126, 133; Meiji, 22, 38; postwar revision of, 58–59, 129; proposed revision of, 122, 123; Shotoku's, 30

Constitution, U.S., 37

Convention of Shimoda, 44

Corporate alliances, U.S.-Japan, 7, 77–78

Cripps, Sir Stafford, 66

Cultural agreement, Soviet-Japanese, 146

Cultural borrowing by Japanese, 73–74; from China, 29–33, 74. *See also* Westernization of Japan

Cultural differences, U.S.-Japan, 19, 22, 23, 163–164

Cultural domination: of Chinese over Japanese people, 150

Cultural ties, U.S.-Japan, 7

Daimyo, 35

Daini Dendem (company), 94

Daiwa ("Great Peace"), 21

Datsun automobile: scoffed at, 49

Debt service, Japanese, 68

Defense buildup, Japanese, 121, 135–136; constraints on, 131–135; during Meiji Restoration, 38; plan for, 135–136

Defense expenditures: Japanese, 12–13, 66, 68, 120, 121, 130–139 passim; U.S., 119, 120

Defense policy, Japanese: and buildup program, 121, 135–136, 139; civilian control of, 128–131; and Constitution's Article 9, 12, 71, 120, 121–122, 126, 133; constraints on, 12–13, 119–127, 131–136; institutional framework of, 127–128; and Mutual Security Treaty, 120, 122–124,

139; and non-nuclear principles, 124–125; and participation in SDI, 136–138, 146–147; and sea-lane defense, 138–139; U.S. as payer for, 173; U.S.-Japan differences over, 12–13, 119–121, 139; U.S.-Japan tensions over, 6, 7, 119, 120–121; U.S.-Japan trade unfairly linked to, 12

Defense technology: U.S.-Japan trade in, 71–72

Defense White Paper, Japanese, 124

Demilitarization. *See* Disarmament

Democratic Party (Japan): merged with Liberal Party, 59

Democrats, U.S.: and industrial policy, 84

Deng Xiaoping, 134, 152

Deshima, 35, 42

Detroit, 79, 81; unemployment in, 77

Diet (Japanese parliament), 9, 38, 59, 61, 123, 124, 133, 138, 157

Digital-Switch Corporation, 94

Diplomatic overtures, U.S.: to Japan, 44–46; 53–57

Disarmament: called for in Japanese Constitution, 8, 12, 13, 59, 71, 120, 121; of citizens, under Hideyoshi, 35

Disasters: in Japan, 5, 20

Dulles, John Foster, 60, 144

Dutch language: in Japan, 37, 44, 66

Dutchmen: in Japan, 35, 42–43, 66

Earthquakes: in Japan, 20

East Asia, 131, 151; Japanese influence in, 48, 174; Japan's military power in, 47, 56; Soviet influence in, 142

East China Sea, 141

East-West relations, 14

Economy of Japan, 65–105; and expansion of domestic demand, 10, 11, 95–98, 100, 117, 120; and need for internationalism and liberalism, 13–14, 70, 88, 168, 172; prewar expansion of, 66, 87; postwar recovery of, 9, 61, 65, 67–68; recent growth in, 100; restructuring proposed, 117; and self-analysis, 166; under Tokugawa, 36–37; and yen-dollar exchange rate, 98–101, 107–108, 110, 114. *See also* Gross National Product (GNP), Japanese; Investments; Savings, Japanese; U.S.-Japan trade

Edo. *See* Tokyo

Education, Japanese, 24; self-, 164; of women, 46

Educational ties, U.S.-Japan, 7

Hawaii: annexed by U.S., 47; Japanese population in, 47
Hay, John, 47
Heavy industries: Sino-Japanese trade in, 152
Heian, 33
Health research: U.S.-Japan cooperation in, 7
Hideyoshi Toytomi, 34; plan to conquer China and Korea, 35, 39
Hierarchies: in Japanese society, 36, 167
Hiragana, 32
Hirohito, Emperor, 19
Hitachi (company), 72, 115; effect of strong yen on, 101
Hitler, Adolf, 52
Hizen, 37
Hokkaido, 21, 23, 26
Holland, 32: and Japan's exclusionist policy, 42–43. *See also* Dutch language; Dutchmen
Honda (company), 109
Honeywell, 104
Hong Kong, 83
Honshu, 37
Hornbeck, Stanley K., 51, 53–54, 56; quoted, 56
Household savings: in Japan, 88–89
Housing, Japanese: construction and purchase encouraged, 96–97
Hughes Communication Company, 93
Hull, Cordell, 50, 51, 54, 55
"Human frontiers" (research program), 170

Iacocca, Lee, 77
Ideographs, Chinese: in Japanese language, 20, 30, 32
Ikeda Hayato, 9, 61
Illinois: Japanese plants in, 115
Immigrants: in U.S., 26, 47–48
Immigration Act, U.S. (1952), 48
Immigration Law, U.S. (1924), 47–48
Imperial Armed Forces, 129
Imperial Japanese Army, 159
Imperial Rescript on Education, 38
Imperial Rule Assistance Association, 52
Imports and exports. *See* U.S.-Japan trade
Income: Japanese per capita, 67
Independence: postwar Japanese, 61–63
Individualism: American stress on, 24; as needed in Japan, 168
Indochina, 56; Japanese forces in, 52, 53

Industrial policy: Japanese, 81–85; U.S., 81, 84, 85
Insularity, Japanese, 13, 19, 20, 25, 163, 165, 173
"Intelligence" sources, British and American: before Pearl Harbor, 56
International fund: Japan's contribution to, 170
Internationalization of Japan: need for, 13–15, 87, 88, 164–175 passim
Internecine warfare: in Japan, 5
Investments, Japanese: competition for, 11, 115–116; in domestic infrastructure, 89–90; overseas, 104, 108, 109 (table), 110, 111, 112–113 (table)
— in U.S.: areas of friction, 111, 114–115; and competition, 115–116; types of, 87, 104, 105, 107, 108–111
Isolationism, U.S., 50
Italy, 170; Fascist, Japan's pact with, 51
Iwakura Tomoni, 46

"Japan-bashing," 6–7, 9, 117
Japan Communist Party (JCP), 59
Japan Defense Agency (JDA), 134, 135, 138, 143; civilian control of, 127, 128, 129–130; weakness of, 13, 121, 126, 131; Japan Development Bank, 83
Japanese Cabinet, 133, 134
Japanese Chamber of Commerce and Industry, 171
Japanese Embassy in Moscow, 146
Japanese Home Ministry, 130
Japanese House of Peers, 38. *See also* Diet
Japanese House of Representatives, 38, 124, 157; Communist seats in, 59. *See also* Diet
Japanese language, 20, 23, 30, 32–33; as barrier in U.S.-Japan relations, 91, 125
Japanese Ministry of Construction, 72
Japanese Ministry of Education, 154, 159
Japanese Ministry of Finance, 83, 98, 116, 126–131 passim
Japanese Ministry of Foreign Affairs, 83, 96, 126, 127, 130
Japanese Ministry of Health and Welfare, 95, 130
Japanese Ministry of International Trade and Industry (MITI), 71, 74, 82, 83, 126, 127, 128, 169, 170; controversial role of, 83; failures of, 83–84
Japanese Ministry of Labor, 108
Japanese National Security Council, 127
Japanese Naval General Staff, 53

Racism: in U.S., 47–48

Rangoon bombings, 14, 174

Raw materials, 55: Japanese import of, 49, 66, 68, 69

RCA Corporation, 93, 115

Reagan, Ronald, 8, 84, 119, 138, 168, 170, 177; and negotiations on U.S.-Japan trade, 91–92, 97, 98

Real estate, U.S.: Japanese investment in, 105, 108–109, 110–111, 115

Rearmament: of Japan urged by U.S., 8, 127. *See also* Defense buildup

Records of Ancient Matters, 20

"Reformers," Japanese, 166, 167–168

Reform in Japan: during Meiji Restoration, 38, 65; postwar, 58–59, 60

Rehabilitation of Japan, 8, 60

Reischauer, Edwin O., 125, 173

Religion in Japan: early, 21–22, 29–30, 32, 33; Christian, 34, 178

Republicans, U.S.: and industrial policy, 84

Republic of China. *See* Taiwan

Republic of Korea (ROK). *See* South Korea

Research and development (R & D): in Japan, 72, 73–74, 82; in U.S., 71, 72, 73, 74; in Western world, 82

Research Council on the Constitution, Japanese, 122

"Returnees" from abroad, Japanese, 167

Rezanov, Count Nikolai Petrovich, 42

"Rhee Line," 158

Riots in Japan (1960), 8–9, 61, 180

Rivalry: between Japan and U.S., 6. *See also* Competition

Roads in Japan: percentage paved, 88

Roberts, Edmund, 41

Robotics: in Japan, 74–76; in U.S., 76

Rogers, William, 148

Roosevelt, Franklin D., 48–49, 50, 54, 55; quoted, 49

R.U.R. (play by Capek), 75

Russia: defeated by Japan, 46; and Japan's exclusionist policy, 42; Perry's attitude toward, 43; post-Revolution (*see* Soviet Union). *See also* Russo-Japanese War

Russo-Japanese Neutrality Pact, 142

Russo-Japanese War (1904–1905), 39, 142, 156

Sakhalin, Southern, 144

Samoan Islands, western: annexed by U.S., 47

Samurai, 33, 37; ethic of, 23, 51; as merchants, 66

"Samurai bonds," 104

Sanctions, economic: proposed against Japan, 50

San Diego, 109

San Francisco Peace Conference, 149

San Francisco Peace Treaty. *See* Peace treaty, U.S.-Japan

Sankin kotai ("attendance by turn"), 35–36

Sansom, Sir George, quoted, 36

Sanyo, 115

Sato, Eisaku, 123, 124

Satsuma, 37

Savings, Japanese, 88–89, 90, 98; outlets needed for, 87–88, 103–104, 105

Savings, U.S.: paucity of, 89

Science and Technology Agency, Japanese, 74

Science Research, 170

Sea lanes, defense of, 124, 132, 138–139

Securities, U.S.: Japanese investment in, 10, 87, 104, 108

Security, comprehensive: doctrine of, 171

Sei-i-Tai-Shogun, 21

Self-Defense Forces (SDF), Japanese, 12, 60, 61, 119, 121, 132, 134, 135, 136; civilian control of, 126, 128, 129; proposed reform of, 136

Self-education, Japanese, 164

Self-image, Japanese, 166

Semi-conductor industry: U.S. vs. Japan in, 73, 83

Semi Conductor Industry Association, 94

Seoul, 157, 159

Seppuku, 57

Sewer systems, modern Japanese: paucity of, 88

Shanghai communique (1972), quoted, 62–63

Sharp Electronics, 115

Shikoku, 37

Shikotan Island, 15, 142, 144

Shimoda, convention of, 44

Shingon sect, 32

Shinto, 20, 21–22, 30, 75, 178; State, abolished, 22, 58; State, formed, 22

Shipbuilding, Japanese, 83, 101

Shogun, 33; first use of title of, 21; Tokugawa as, 34, 35–36, 37, 45

Shogun (Clavell), 35

Shotoku, Prince, 29–30

Shultz, George, 94

Siberia, 51, 142, 143, 147, 154